Esmé

Guardian of Snowdonia

Esmé

Guardian of Snowdonia

Teleri Bevan

First impression: 2014
Second impression: 2016

Cover design: Y Lolfa

Thanks to Jennifer Tillay, Valerie Collett, Geraint Roberts and
Judy Greaves for the use of the photographs

ISBN: 978 184771 955 3

Published and printed in Wales
on paper from well-maintained forests by
Y Lolfa Cyf., Talybont, Ceredigion SY24 5HE
website www.ylolfa.com
e-mail ylolfa@ylolfa.com
tel 01970 832 304
fax 832 782

Foreword

R ARELY DID THE writer of a biography and her subject fit each other so appropriately as Teleri Bevan and Esmé, which is why I am delighted to write a foreword, out of respect and admiration for both.

I was introduced to Esmé in the early 1950s by my father, a hill-walking Presbyterian minister in the Conwy Valley, whose well-annotated copy of Thomas Firbank's autobiography, *I Bought a Mountain*, I treasure among my books on Eryri Snowdonia. I had to wait until the 1990s before meeting the author himself through his daughter Johanna when he came back to stay nearby at Dolwyddelan, over the mountain from Dyffryn Mymbyr.

In between times I came to work closely with Esmé, though always in awe of her, and enjoyed the warm friendship of Peter Kirby. The strengths of these three characters and their shared passions are treated sensitively and honestly in this memoir, brought again to life so graphically by Teleri.

Having lived all my life around Eryri Snowdonia, I have no doubt that such landscapes produce very special people. To love and live in a mountain landscape whether as hill-farmer, botanist, climber or outdoor instructor, is to pursue a determined lifestyle with undoubted economic sacrifices made for other less direct benefits.

Visitors over generations who have found the climate and culture of such areas incomprehensible, if not threatening, will always have great difficulty in appreciating why people who love such landscapes do so with such determined ferocity.

Where long geological time is so close to the surface, the pressing need for change in each generation will always generate deep-seated arguments. Yet those like Esmé, who campaigned seemingly against change, also enabled it to happen in a more sustainable way. Today, at Hafod y Llan and Llyndy Isaf, the National Trust champions renewable energy and sustainable agriculture for young entrants, while providing access and landscape conservation 'for ever' on Esmé's beloved Dyffryn Mymbyr.

Lord Dafydd Elis-Thomas PC AM
August 2014

Introduction

E SMÉ CAUGHT HER first glimpse of Dyffryn on the day of her wedding. She saw the sturdy house where she was to live for the rest of her life.

She had married Thomas Joseph Firbank that morning, 22 March 1934, at a parish church in Chester. She'd then been whisked away to Snowdonia, to a mountain farmhouse perched two hundred feet above the road, on Glyder Fach.

Thomas and Esmé had fallen deeply in love and, with their impetuous natures, they'd married following a passionate courtship of two or three months. They were both twenty-three years old.

Three years earlier, on his return from Canada, Thomas had bought Dyffryn, a mountain farm of 2,400 acres, despite having no farm experience. Esmé didn't have a farming background either, for she had been at drama school in London.

Their experiences at Dyffryn in the late 1930s were chronicled by Thomas Firbank in his international bestselling book, *I Bought a Mountain*, published in 1940. During the Second World War Thomas joined up with the Coldstream Guards, and chose never to return to Dyffryn.

Esmé remained on the farm, supported by two shepherds and two sheepdogs. She lived in a caravan and let the house out to a family from south-east England who was escaping wartime bombing raids. She was determined to make Dyffryn one of the best mountain farms in Wales and, with advice and help during the tough times from her neighbours in Snowdonia, she became a skilled hands-on farmer. Towards the end of the war she met Major Peter Kirby who was in command of Sandhurst's battle camp at Capel Curig. They married in 1947.

Snowdonia became a National Park in 1951 and Esmé, as a working farmer within the Park, grew more and more interested in conservation. In 1967 she established what she termed a watchdog, an independent body, and named it the Snowdonia National Park Society. Its aims were to protect the mountains from commercial developers and the impact of the thousands of tourists attracted to its tranquillity. The Society became a passion for Esmé, a lady who was forthright and direct in the way she led the organisation. She enthused and inspired over 3,000 people to join the Society, to work voluntarily for the protection of a unique, rugged landscape.

I visited Esmé at Dyffryn one frosty January morning in 1978 in the company of broadcaster and conservationist, Wynford Vaughan-Thomas, who knew Esmé well. They talked of climbing heroes; he'd recently read the biography of the London Welshman, O.G. Jones, who '... had the arms of a gorilla, and he had burst like a bombshell into the closed society of dons, civil servants, public schoolmen and businessmen who were then the guardian of climbing tradition.' O.G. upset the Establishment in the 1880s by pushing for the development of a climbing technique beyond the perceived safe limits of the day. Wynford himself was not a natural rock climber; however we were planning later that spring a nine-day walk of over two hundred miles from south Wales to the north, but not on tracks, paths or roads, but on the 'roof of Wales'. It was a route that he'd designed himself. He would then broadcast his exploits on a half-hour programme on Radio 4 each morning. And he was also celebrating his seventieth birthday that year!

Esmé reflected on his 'adventure' during our short visit over a glass of sloe gin to 'warm ourselves'. Both talked of the constant pressure on the hills and mountains of Snowdonia, showing a deep concern for the landscape of Wales. While Esmé had motivated herself to establish a Society, Wynford was vice-president of the then Council for the Protection of Rural Wales (CPRW). Both were natural communicators who crystallised their beliefs and never relinquished.

Esmé life's work was inimitable for its campaigning and creativeness. Her long life brought about many successes in conserving the landscape of Snowdonia for us to enjoy today.

Teleri Bevan
September 2014

Acknowledgements

THERE ARE MANY who have given me different insights into the life and work of Esmé Kirby. I am truly grateful for their time and observations. The following are not in any order of importance but are knowledgeable commentators on aspects of the life and work of Esmé.

Jennifer Tillay and Valerie Collett, Esmé's nieces – they and their husbands gave me letters and recalled their youthful memories of long holidays at Dyffryn; Roger Cummins, nephew; Geraint Roberts, the tenant and farmer of Dyffryn; Jane Pullee, Pen-y-Gwryd Hotel; John Disley, president of the Snowdonia Society; David Firth, chairman of the Snowdonia Society (retired); Caerwyn Roberts, farmer and chairman of the Snowdonia National Park Authority; John Morgan, acting director Wales National Trust; Alan Jones, Snowdonia National Park officer (retired); Bob Lowe, Countryside Council (retired) and member of the Snowdonia Society committee; Richard Williams Ellis, Jeremy Williams Ellis and Helen Owen, Glasfryn Estate; Elizabeth Williams Ellis; Richard Williams, who farmed Hafod y Llan; Emyr Williams, director of the Snowdonia National Park Authority; Edna Jones, farmer; Dr Craig Shuttleworth, director Red Squirrel Trust Wales; Gareth Clubb, director of the Snowdonia Society (2009–11); Harvey Lloyd, secretary of the Snowdonia Society (retired); Elizabeth Colwyn-Foulkes, chairman of the Campaign for the Protection of Rural Wales (retired); Dei Thomas, environmentalist and broadcaster; Gunna Chown, Bodegroes Hotel; Richard Prichard, Royal Welch

11

Fusiliers Museum, Caernarfon; Judy Greaves, sculptor of the memorial seat overlooking Dyffryn Mymbyr.

My gratitude to Lord Dafydd Elis-Thomas for his wonderful Foreword.

And for advice and care from Eirian Jones of Y Lolfa, the publishers.

And a special 'Thank you' to Claire and the family for being a constant support.

Diolch yn fawr i chi gyd.

1

E SMÉ WAS BORN to be centre stage, but not as an actor, but as a woman who cared passionately for a cause – the Snowdonia landscape where she lived and farmed for almost seventy years. Short and diminutive in stature, she was nevertheless a commanding presence: attractive, well groomed in bright colours – usually red; her make-up highlighting her high cheekbones and sparkling eyes. When she spoke on a public platform, people listened. Her speeches for campaigns were well-researched and constructed, not over-long, and the message clear and to the point. Her mission was to keep the Snowdonia National Park free from development and commercialisation.

Thomas Firbank's first impression of Esmé when he caught his first glimpse of her in a town street is noted in his bestselling book, 'She was small, lithe, with a hard slim body and the face of an elf. She was as dainty as a Dresden shepherdess.' It was 1934 and within a week they were engaged and later secretly married at the Church of St John the Baptist, Chester. Not one representative of their families or any friends were present at the ceremony – their witnesses were two people they'd met the previous evening. Following the nuptials and a thank you drink, they made their way towards the Conwy Valley and Capel Curig. Their life together began in the heart of the Snowdon massif where, in 1931, Thomas had impetuously bought a 2,400-acre hill farm called Dyffryn.

Dyffryn was typical of many mountain farms. Remote and rugged, their home was a solid stone house perched above the Dyffryn Mymbyr Valley. It was five miles from Capel Curig, the wettest place in the land according to weather forecasters. Their mountain was Glyder Fach, conjoined to her 'big sister' Glyder Fawr, known together as the Glyderau, and both over 3,000 feet high. The mountains seemed threatening, with their steep scree slopes often rising into dark clouds from Dyffryn's back door – the rocky terrain the result of glacial activity during the Ice Age. Directly across the valley from the house were the greener slopes of Moel Siabod. The valley which links Moel Siabod with the Glyderau is Dyffryn Mymbyr; it's five miles long with the River Mymbyr flowing towards two lakes, Llynnau Mymbyr, and the village of Capel Curig. But the dominant vista from Dyffryn is the familiar horseshoe contour of Snowdon, the highest in a range of fourteen mountains extending over 3,000 feet in the area.

Esmé came to understand and love this dramatic landscape over the years, but farming these mountains was a very robust challenge. The farm had a flock of around six hundred sheep and a small herd of store cattle. As the sun's rays warmed the soil, the grass turned from brown to bright green, with the grazing land being at the floor of the valley close to the river. Later in the year this area was the only source of decent grass for haymaking, a task so dependent on the weather – three dry sunny days in succession would just about be sufficient to mow, dry and carry the hay back to the barn near the road.

The 1930s were years of deep economic troubles, prices slumped and earning a living from wild, rugged rocky terrain like Snowdonia was hard graft. There was little money for investment, although in the three years since he'd bought Dyffryn, Thomas Firbank had improved the house a little. By now there was running water and a range, but it would take until the end of the decade before there was electricity in the house. At this time many farmers sold up and gave up the struggle; others in turn were able to increase their acreage of land, but the first major agricultural study of Snowdonia, published in 1949 by the eminent geologist F.J. North, concluded:

> Prices collapsed and the loss of skilled labour and capital in the 1930s resulted in failure to keep up the land management required for the successful breeding of ewes and lambs. It has been suggested that it is difficult to make a reasonable living out of sheep farming at the present time with a flock of less than a thousand sheep, and one rough estimate gave figures that there were only some hundred flocks of this size in the whole of Wales.

Statistical evidence by Emyr Williams, former director of land management at the Snowdonia National Park Authority, illustrates the rate of change in the mountains over the years. He calculated that at the end of the nineteenth century there were almost 3,000 farms in Snowdonia. By the 1960s the number had dropped to 1,800, and as the new millennium dawned, 1,200, and by the end of the first decade in 2010, only 1,000 remained actively working. Many were forced to diversify and adapt and, as farms came onto the market, this land was often bought up by other farmers to create bigger and more viable units.

Thomas Firbank also rented land from a neighbouring farm, but not until the late 1930s when the economic problems had eased somewhat. The tenant farmer of Cwm Ffynnon at that time, Price Williams, was giving up and, as the land bordered with Dyffryn on the Glyder Fawr side, there were fine possibilities. The nearly 1,000-acre Cwm Ffynnon farm was likened to a deep bowl, its sides in the form of wide cliffs reaching down to the Llanberis Pass. The farm's attraction was good grazing, plenty of heather, whin and mountain grass, and enough grazing for about six hundred sheep. They believed it could be a 'goldmine', so they rented it and increased their farming land substantially.

Thomas and Esmé attempted to increase their income by diversifying their production too at that time. They kept poultry, but that ended in tragedy because of rampant disease. The pig project was too labour intensive and uneconomic. So, they turned to operating a snack bar on the main road to take advantage of passing tourists. July and August were really busy times, and even the shepherds were involved in serving customers and washing up, but it became clear that their small returns weren't worth the effort. The snack bar experiment prompted Esmé to think of erecting a more permanent wooden structure. And it was at that time that she began to wonder what would happen to their lovely valley with the increasing influx of tourists. They then bought a caravan in Birmingham and it was towed home on a perilous journey with Thomas, the shepherd, sitting inside the caravan along the winding roads and lanes of Wales.

In the spring of 1939 Thomas and Esmé separated. No official reason was given, but Thomas wrote in his second book, *I Bought a Star*, 'The gap widened between Esmé and me, until neither of us could bridge it.' Esmé, however, kept her own counsel, never voicing her own agony in public, but rumours in a close-knit community travelled around the valleys at wild speed.

Esmé faced the busiest time in the farming year; there was no time to dwell on recent events. The first challenges would be haymaking, and separating lambs from ewes was necessary. Her family living in Deganwy begged her to give up and return to the coast. But Dyffryn was now her home. She had a stubborn streak, she had invested too much energy, stamina and love in the farm and she had learnt so much about hill farming practices and sheep husbandry in five years. She was not about to give up; the neighbours were helpful, and the shepherds, father and son John and Thomas Davies, and the sheep dogs Luck and Mot were loyal and hard working.

Thomas never returned to Dyffryn. He drove away in his Bentley called Arabella to the Pyrenees mountains between France and Spain, where he wrote of his farming experiences and his romance and marriage in the book, *I Bought a Mountain*. When the Second World War was declared in September 1939, he raced from Spain to England to submit the completed manuscript to the publishers Harrap & Co. Published in 1940, it remains the iconic chronicle of the ups and downs of newcomers to the rigour of mountain farming in Snowdonia. Firbank later joined the army, becoming a lieutenant colonel and he saw service in North Africa and Italy. He won the Military Cross and became an instructor for two years after the armistice in 1945.

They had both moved on, on different paths. Esmé loved farming but found the going tough and Dyffryn remained challenging. Thomas Firbank was the restless observer, 'Anticipation is a spur, realisation an anti-climax,' he wrote in his second publication, *I Bought a Star*. Esmé? She became Snowdonia's guardian. She transferred her love and romance for one man to a passion for the mountains, and this is her story.

2

WHEN I BEGAN researching this book I met Esmé's close family members, nieces Jenny and Val, her sister's daughters, and I asked them who had been the greatest influence on Esmé's life and career. Without hesitation, they answered in unison, 'Her father'.

Tancred Disraeli Cummins was a cavalier businessman, a risk-taker and a traveller who came originally from Manchester. His family was involved in the cotton industry but, as a young man, Tancred sought a career at the Manchester Stock Exchange, hoping to make his own fortune. His parents must have felt a sense of destiny when their second son was born – his name ensured certain notoriety, in honour of Prime Minister Benjamin Disraeli, the reforming statesman and novelist. *Tancred* was the title of the first of his three novels, published in 1847. The novel was based on the theme of a crusade searching for reconciliation between Judaism and Christianity. The subtitle 'The New Crusade' was taken from the novel's idealistic hero, Tancred, as he retraced a journey to the Holy Land in order to understand the roots of Christianity.

During his time in the world of finance Tancred was asked by a young disabled relative whether he could accompany him on a journey around the world. He'd be paid handsomely for the assistance and company, enough to set up him up in a business on his return. Without hesitation Tancred agreed; he was young and unmarried and this would be an adventure of a lifetime. The journey took a year but, before they parted, another world tour was arranged – this time, to follow another geographical latitude line around the world. In fact he was paid handsomely for three successful year-long journeys, but his many business ventures were financially underpinned by his indulgent father.

Just before his last world tour, Tancred met Dora, his prospective wife who was almost twenty years younger than him. He fell deeply in love with Dora; they would live in Surrey where he proposed to set up a business designing golf courses. Having bought a plot of land in Addington, near Croydon, he designed and built a large house and filled it with figures and artefacts he'd collected on his travels. He designed the Addington Court golf course which was opened in 1907 and it was a profitable venture in such a prosperous area. His other line of business was holding patents, and they ranged from a worm cast collector to a teeing mat and a shoe rack. He remained a member of the Manchester Stock Exchange and his involvement in the cotton business continued.

Dora came from a distinguished family of artists. Her father, John Anderson Hague, trained at the Manchester Academy of Fine Art and he was soon influenced by the prior actions of his father, Joshua, who in his youth and as a student of the Academy had led a rebellion of students. They consistently refused to conform to the School of Art's rules and decided to develop their own style and to establish studios in the Conwy Valley. This group of painters was eventually recognised as the Royal Cambrian Academy, a formidable influence in the art world.

With the prospect of the First World War becoming closer and danger in south-east England becoming a real threat, Tancred took the decision to move to north Wales to escape the Zeppelin raids. He sold the Addington Court golf course. Today it is a world-class course and was later redesigned by the renowned architect, John Frederick Abercrombie. Peter Allis once described it as a 'wonderful oasis'.

Dora was grateful to return to the familiar surroundings of north Wales. They bought a large, sunny house in Deganwy, close to Llandudno, and this became their permanent home. Tancred would have to travel regularly to deal with his business interests in London and Manchester, but he had already invested earlier in north Wales. He had seen suitable land for sale during Christmas 1893 when the family spent the holiday with Dora's family. He went on to buy a strip of the Conwy estuary coastline, Penmorfa Beach on Llandudno's west shore, from the Church commissioners. It was the perfect location, with its sand dunes and hills, for a golf links course. It also boasted glorious views of the Conwy estuary, had the backdrop of the Snowdonia mountains and, in the distance, the town of Beaumaris on Anglesey. Tancred relied on the advice of two experienced golfers for the layout of the course: John Ball, the Open amateur golf champion and Harold Hinton, the Open champion. A year later, in 1894, the nine-hole Llandudno Golf Club was opened and it soon metamorphosed into the eighteen-hole North Wales Golf Club which hosted many championships. Tancred was the Club's captain and secretary until 1933, working tirelessly to increase its membership. For an area developing as a successful holiday resort, it proved a worthy attraction for visitors.

Tancred had given a name to each hole on the course: the thirteenth short hole, playing directly into the prevailing wind, was called 'Hades', but the Church commissioners requested that the name be changed as it was inappropriate with land previously connected to the Church. Tancred refused, but in order to placate their displeasure, he named the eighteenth hole, 'Paradise'. Obstinacy, coupled with amusing mischief, was a trait he handed down to his daughter Esmé.

Tancred and Dora's children became involved in golf as soon as Club rules allowed. Daughters Doreen, Esméralda (Esmé) and Eileen were very keen and became the Club's first three junior members. Esmé had a natural aptitude for sport: she was on the course almost every day and her handicap dropped to twelve. She was entered in all competitive championships, losing the ladies' championship by a small margin at the age of just fourteen.

Golf was not her only sport; she excelled at gymnastics, netball, hockey and tennis, becoming a County tennis player. She also had a growing interest in amateur dramatics and wildlife. She would often spot an injured bird or stray and take them back to her bedroom and nurture them back to health. Esmé was also interested in literature, history and the arts. She would quote poems in her writing to emphasise the range of her interest in literature, or to illustrate a point she was making.

She was part of a large family of four girls and two boys who were educated in private boarding schools. Guy, the eldest, and Michael were educated at Wrekin College, Shropshire. The four girls, Doreen, Esmé, Eileen and June were educated at Arne Hall School, in Llandudno. The children did well at school, but only one went to university. Doreen wanted to be a geography teacher. She received her degree from Bedford College, London, then taught in York before meeting her prospective husband who worked in the Colonial office and was later posted to Barbados. Guy became a chartered surveyor. Michael joined the Chloride Battery Company in Manchester before joining the army; he was awarded the MBE and died in 1944. Eileen moved to

Bowden, Cheshire, and became a homemaker as did June, the youngest.

Esmé was the naughty one, beguiling maybe, but in school she was a gang leader. She may have excelled at all sports but, when she brought one or two games into the classroom, such as throwing an inkwell at a surprised teacher and calling 'Catch!', the punishment was immediate. She was banned from games. Her mother was incensed, but Esmé was soon up to her antics again and eventually she was suspended. She'd meant no malice, just fun. Tancred was, as ever, lenient and indulgent.

But it was an appearance in a school play that was the turning point in her young life. Arne Hall School encouraged her to do drama in an attempt to channel her rebellious nature – even at her young age she seemed so assured, had presence and could interpret character and emotion. Teachers were ever-watchful of her headstrong manner. Acting therefore became her favourite subject; she liked dressing up, the more exotic the costume and wig, the more Esmé liked being someone else. Despite her lack of physical stature, she made up for it with amazing personal energy. Her grandfather had once given her the family signet ring with one word written on it, 'courage', and that seemed to sum Esmé up.

The name of the play and the part that she played has been lost in the mists of time, but sitting in the audience at one of the school's performances was an agent of the celebrated actor and manager, Sir Frank Benson. He was so impressed at her potential that he immediately spoke to her teachers and parents, suggesting that the seventeen-year-old Esmé could be invited to join his acting school. Esmé was thrilled. There were many parental discussions: Dora was anxious; Tancred, the risk-taker, was not so concerned.

F.R. Benson was an important influence in contemporary theatre at the time. Occasionally there would be as many as three repertory companies travelling around Britain, and these included many actors and actresses trained by him. His acting school had been established in 1901. He was the first to produce the cycle of English history plays on the stage and had developed and pioneered the Stratford-upon-Avon Shakespeare Festival.

During Esmé's interview and audition he perceived a lively but self-contained young lady who could easily fit into life 'on the boards'. Esmé could also add another dimension to the company, her interest in sport. Sir Frank was also a sporty type and believed that all actors ought to keep fit. During interviews he was constantly looking for students who could be members of his hockey, cricket, and tennis teams.

Benson was a colourful character. The Shakespearean fights and duels on stage took twice the time necessary because Sir Frank would throw himself into acrobatic action, bounding on tables, flashing his sword with flamboyant and exaggerated movements, just like a man possessed. His eccentricity went as far as cracking the ice on a pond near the theatre, diving into the water, and going swimming between the matinee of *Hamlet* and the evening performance of *Richard III*. However, at times, his mannerisms and exaggerated speech of mangled words turned the text into an incomprehensible rhythmic dirge.

The Benson Company was among the best schools of acting for providing opportunities to budding actors. Sir Frank was an effective and charismatic leader and was given a knighthood on the Drury Lane stage in 1916 after a performance of *Julius Caesar*, for his work in setting up the acclaimed Shakespeare Festival and for giving many actors their first opportunities.

The work of the theatre company was often exhausting but, in the main, it was exhilarating. No two days were the same and no two performances were exactly alike. Esmé was given small parts in a few productions and, whenever possible, she found time to see other London productions too. There was much to learn, not only acting techniques. She also got to know more about working backstage behind the scenes – stage managing, assisting wardrobe and props, being a runner or a prompter, making endless cups of tea. Whatever she did, she threw herself into every aspect. It was almost a life of make-believe, but reality unfortunately soon set in.

She caught an infection which was diagnosed as mumps. She was sent home to Deganwy, but her recovery was slow and painful. Her mother prevailed on her to stay at home until she regained her strength. Her aspirations for an acting career had taken a knock, but as she began to recuperate, she learnt to ride properly and also to teach others. Thomas Firbank came to that school for riding lessons. Within a few weeks they'd married. For Esmé, it was another major turning point in her life.

3

I N MANY RESPECTS the five years between 1934 and 1939 were happy years at Dyffryn. They were fulfilling, full of incident and adventure, and chronicled vividly by Thomas in his book *I Bought a Mountain*. But the early years were hard for Esmé and, when Thomas left, it became much tougher, physically and emotionally.

There was little money and Esmé knew that if she was to survive she would have to look seriously at her spending and at how to generate extra income. As noted, it was not the best of times, hill farm incomes dropped in the 1930s, with the price of wool and sheep slumping.

Farmers who worked in the mountains of Snowdonia used the same farming husbandry practices as handed down through the generations. Changing these practices on unfenced, difficult land was almost impossible – livestock had been bred to remain enclosed within the rugged boundaries, finding their grazing areas among rocks and, in winter, making their way towards hereditary shelters from the storms and snow. Esmé learned to respect these inherited customs and the traits of 'hefted flocks'. Using her understanding and ingenuity, she became a proficient hill farmer, and earned the respect of her peers and her neighbours. She was courageous in accepting the formidable challenge of farming the mountain on her own.

Still young, not yet thirty, the banks would not easily allow a young woman on her own to borrow money, especially in those years of economic turmoil. So the need to find another source of income and cash flow was critical. Within days of Thomas leaving, Esmé decided that she'd move out of the main house, let it to a tenant, and then move into the caravan parked close to the barn as soon as that could be made habitable and comfortable, with her bathroom being a deep pool in the River Mymbyr in both summer and winter.

Dyffryn house was a solid dwelling built of stone in the early nineteenth century and had been a part of the Penrhyn Estate. It was surrounded by trees which had withstood many a storm over the decades. These trees are the only ones in the valley and no-one seems to know their age. The west-facing wall of the house was clad with hung slate, the most effective way of resisting the lashing rain and storms. Inside the house and overlooking the valley were two large sitting rooms, either side of the hallway, and a kitchen and two pantries at the back. Thomas had reduced the six bedrooms to four to accommodate a bathroom, and downstairs he had also created a smaller sitting area near the kitchen.

Also there stood a smaller house behind, built in the thirteenth century, and just as solid as the main house. It had one big room which had a large fireplace at one end, low beams, small windows, and three bedrooms. It was built like a manor but was not really habitable at that time. There were two other cottages too, about two hundred feet down a narrow track towards the main road between Capel Curig and Llanberis. They were built of stone, with the purple Caernarfon slate on the roof. At one time they'd been the homes of quarrymen, but were now occupied by the shepherds. Across the main road lay a cluster of farm buildings, barns and sheds, with the gates and some of the doors painted in a distinctive pale green colour.

The meadows on the banks of the River Mymbyr were kept for grazing and haymaking in the spring and summer. These meadows weren't ideal for haymaking, as large patches were marshy ground. Past generations had cleared many boulders and large stones from the meadows to avoid damaging modern mowing and other haymaking machines.

Dry-stone walls enclosed a 600-acre enclosure, the *ffridd*, on the Glyderau, where the flock was managed at the time of gathering or shearing. Some dry-stone walls on the higher ground of Snowdonia were six hundred years old, but the majority were built around two hundred years ago. These six to seven feet high, and two feet thick walls are invaluable for protecting livestock.

Above the enclosed *ffridd* was the open mountain where the core Welsh Mountain sheep had an inherent knowledge of boundaries, sheep walks and paths handed down from ewe to lamb. Wild goats also lived permanently in the higher reaches, their agility to leap from crag to crag in search of food or to find shelter admirable, a feat that put sheep to shame.

To help with managing her flock, Esmé had two experienced shepherds, John and Thomas Davies. Two faithful sheepdogs, Luck and Mot, were on hand too. The hill farmer's working year was long and tiring. A watchful eye had to be kept on the flock for signs of disease, and the actions of predators, such as foxes and crows, made lambs vulnerable. Every sheep or lamb lost was costly to the overall income at the end of the year. At the time of Thomas's departure the lambing had finished and the barren yearling ewes, who'd spent the winter on lowland pastures, had returned to Dyffryn for the summer. The two-year-old ewes had already given birth, and their new-born lambs were now in the meadows alongside the river, close to the barns. The older ewes were in the enclosed *ffridd*.

Hoping and praying for a spell of sunny weather, the

next task for Esmé would be haymaking, then washing and dipping all the sheep, counting the numbers in the flock, later separating the ewes from their lambs and finally, putting the rams in with the two-year-old ewes ready for next year's group of lambs. Then, the most important event of all, the farm's autumn sheep sale.

Many of the farm tasks required additional help, and traditionally neighbours in the community depended on each other for activities such as gathering the flock off the mountain, dipping and washing, shearing, and occasionally, at haymaking time. Farmers or shepherds from Garth, Wern, Cwm Ffynnon, Hen Blas, Pen-y-Bont and Pantyffynnon would regularly come to help Esmé.

They certainly admired Esmé for her commitment to farming. Despite her slight appearance she could handle sheep, even the biggest rams – some bigger than her – taking her turn with the old-fashioned clippers at shearing time, before returning to the house to host lunch for all the shearers and wool packers. She learned quickly how to judge quality animals, appreciating tips from experienced farmers who knew the joys and dangers of working in the mountains and with the native Welsh Mountain, a breed that has a wild quality in their genes coupled with toughness, nimbleness and cunning.

She was the only woman farmer for miles around. She worked hard, occasionally in extreme conditions, when the weather turned to winter. As a youngster, Caerwyn Roberts, now chairman of the Snowdonia National Park Authority, remembers her at the Capel Curig autumn sheep sales bringing her sheep from Dyffryn in a rickety old lorry. She'd separate the rams from ewes, lifting animals from one pen to the next, revealing she had strength and stamina in abundance. At the end of the day when she'd return home, she'd count the money and then pay her shepherds and her debts.

A glimpse of Esmé's life at that time was written in a letter sent to her by S.C. Wells. Inspired after reading *I Bought a Mountain*, he spent a long holiday with his mother nearby one summer at the beginning of the Second World War. He had farmed for many years and was captivated by Esmé's role as written in the book:

> Very few people will be able to appreciate the amount of book-keeping, clerical work, visits to markets and outlying farms to purchase and sell rams, cattle etc. She works with two men from dawn to dusk and, in spite of her slight physique, she can beat most men in a hard day's work such is her strength and endurance. She has let the farmhouse and lives alone in the caravan on the bank of the river in which she bathes daily, in the icy cold waters from Snowdon. On a big rock are her sponge, toothbrush, paste and other toilet articles. She can talk most intelligently on any subject and has a great sense of humour. She does not smoke, drinks only when out enjoying herself; at other times only water, but neither tea nor coffee, and this is a sample of her daily menu: breakfast – apple and cold water; lunch – bread and cheese, apple, cold water; supper – an egg. Chocolates with all three, if available. She reads late into the night; five hours sleep is good enough for her. No trials, losses or disasters upset her. 'What's the use? I just do my best and let it go at that.' Age 29, generally looks 16.

And then a memory of her at work:

> She thinks of nothing of starting off at daybreak to drive a flock of sheep (she owns 3,000) any distance of up to twenty miles, with the aid of two dogs and then, hitch-hike home. She can ride anything on four legs. She can drive any car (power sufficient) up any mountain track provided she can keep two wheels on the ground at the same time. (These are the words of the garage man when we enquired if it was safe to lend her our car to drive home in the blackout, her own being in dock.)

The stories of her cars, vans or lorries are legion, and her driving was in a class of its own. Apparently she spent most of the time looking at the countryside rather than at the road ahead. Passengers held their breath as Esmé gave a running commentary on the landscape. The sight of flocks of sheep grazing the high slopes in high summer occasionally made her stretch her body across the passenger seat to get a better view. While trying to change gear at the same time as approaching a steep hill, she'd notice the quality of flocks and grazing pastures, while being totally unaware of the terror she was causing her passengers in the car. As she was small, she often could not see through the windscreen, so she found many ingenious ways of elevating herself. Cushions, pillows or folded blankets were used, but one of the more permanent structures was made from chicken wire, folded with difficulty into a frame and placed within a pile of sacks. A square piece of foam replaced the sacks when it became cheap and available.

At the end of her first year of farming alone, there were gains and losses. The winter of 1940 had been relatively kind and the autumn sale had been successful. Esmé felt much more confident about the future.

4

A N INITIAL PIECE of good fortune for Esmé came when the contract of the farmhouse's first tenant came to an end. A new advert brought applicants from London who wanted safe havens for their wives and chidren for an extended period. The rent would be £5 a week, a steady income. Esmé was now able to comfortably pay the wages of her shepherds, John and Thomas Davies, and she had a little left for herself each week. However, a few months later, came some bad news – the two shepherds had seen an advertisement for workers at a poultry farm in Cheshire with a wage of five shillings a week, more than they were earning at Dyffryn. It was a wrench for them to leave, but the extra money was a necessity. They had been Dyffryn employees for many years, were loyal and dependable and understood the capricious nature of the mountains.

Indeed Thomas, the son, accompanied Esmé on the 'record walk', the famous mountain challenge known as the Welsh 3000s, which involves traversing in one go the fourteen peaks of Snowdonia which reach a height of over 3,000 feet: Yr Wyddfa/Snowdon, Crib y Ddysgl, Crib Goch, Elidir Fawr, Y Garn, Glyder Fawr, Glyder Fach, Tryfan, Pen yr Ole Wen, Camedd Dafydd, Carnedd Llywelyn, Yr Elen, Foel Grach and Foel Fras. Thomas, her husband, and his companion, completed the walk in August 1938 in eight hours and twenty-five minutes, beating the record by two hours and four minutes. Esmé and Thomas took nine hours and twenty-nine minutes, an hour less than the record despite Esmé's painful limp from a strained ligament in her leg. Their accomplishment was photographed for the centre pages of many national newspapers.

Many tasks on the farm became overdue. She set out a long-term plan for repairing fences, walls and buildings, and also increasing and improving the quality of the sheep flock. She wrote in one letter at this time, 'To some it may seem as hard work, but to me it was a challenge, an exciting adventure and I loved every moment. My ambition was to make Dyffryn the best hill farm in Wales but I soon realised that neither I nor Dyffryn had the necessary qualifications.'

But Esmé soon learnt to enhance her knowledge by seeking advice not only from local farmers but also from the staff of the department of agriculture at University College Wales, Bangor, and the newly-formed government organisation, National Agricultural Advisory Service (NAADS). She also needed time and money to execute these plans, and many locally doubted her nerve and stamina and questioned whether she was all talk.

During the next few years, however, she proved her mettle. Among her helpful farming neighbours was David Jones of Gwastad Annas, who lived in the next valley, Nant Gwynant. When he realised that she was alone, he was impressed with her attitude. David Jones gave her advice and came to help at the gathering and shearing days, and when he went shopping, he would buy a bagful of goods for Esmé, and leave it at the caravan. He was a good friend and a good farmer. And she in turn was heard to say, 'He doesn't crack empty nuts!'

She sought advice especially when the sheep sales approached. In addition to selling, she would hope to buy. It was imperative to buy excellent rams to improve the quality of the flock – they would pass on certain characteristics, although it is difficult to find uniformity in the Welsh

Mountain breed because of a wide range of management regimes and differing geographical locations. In Snowdonia there is high rainfall, difficult terrain and a lack of lush pastures. The one essential characteristic of the breed is hardiness, an ability to withstand cold temperatures and rain. The birth of twins is not welcome in a mountainous environment. Single lambs are the priority; they are sturdier, especially if the ewe has been given extra nutritious food prior to lambing. There are several types of Welsh Mountain sheep depending on the terrain, and to identify the differences farmers formed a society in 1946 to identify them, in time recording improved quality. The ram sale at Capel Curig grew in importance and was the focal point for sharing information and good practice.

Improvement in the stock, however, took years and gradually over a period of ten or fifteen years, the flock at Dyffryn increased in number and quality, a sign that Esmé had listened to advice and bought wisely. The price of young rams had risen and the demand for wool had increased during and after the war, despite Welsh Mountain wool not being of the highest quality: tough, not soft, but hard-wearing and good for rugs and carpets. In 1950 the Wool Marketing Board was established, stabilising the trade by securing markets and achieving the best possible return for producers.

* * *

Sometime during the Second World War Esmé met Major Edward Lisle Kirby who had been posted to Sandhurst's battle camp at Capel Curig (nowadays this is Plas y Brenin, the UK National Mountain Centre). Major Kirby was known as Peter, a nickname he was given at school. He was a

Yorkshireman who'd attended public school in Shrewsbury, followed by a year studying civil engineering at Durham University, before turning to chartered surveying. In 1937 he'd joined the Fourth Battalion Green Howards Territorial Army and, at the outbreak of the Second World War, he was called to full-time service. Later evacuated from Dunkirk, he then took part in the conflict in the Western Desert, where he was taken seriously ill with the effects of sun blindness while commanding a mobile column of infantry, tanks and artillery. He returned to England, and when he recovered he was posted as an instructor to the wartime officer training unit at Sandhurst, and later Sandhurst's battle camp at Capel Curig where he served until the end of the war.

Esmé and Peter met often and she was becoming well known as a result of the success of her husband's book. She liked the attention, although not when she was caught in dungarees and boots. Every so often she would dress up, use her make-up, especially eye shadow and mascara, and spend the evening with Peter in the soft lights of the Royal Hotel at Capel Curig. Since the early nineteenth century, this had been a well-known meeting place for well-heeled visitors who enjoyed walking and climbing, among them Queen Victoria and King George V.

Peter and Esmé soon found many common interests. He visited Dyffryn and saw the conditions in which Esmé lived and worked; he offered to help make the smaller house at the back habitable. By the end of the war she could afford to move out of the caravan and live in the main house again, but it needed many repairs. Peter, who was a gifted artisan, 'set about making the house more comfortable for her,' according to Edna Jones who came to work for Esmé on the farm in 1954.

Edna came from Cheshire, from an upper middle-class

family. She'd worked on a dairy farm and had followed a bacteriology course at a farm college and now, to complete her agricultural education, she needed experience on a hill farm.

'I saw this advertisement in the paper for help on a hill farm. I answered it and Esmé came to Liverpool to interview all the applicants. I think I was the first to go in and she said to me there and then, "Come back with us, come tonight, you've got the job," and then she paused. I said yes and she promptly dismissed all the other candidates, and I experienced for the first time Esmé's driving.'

Edna's eyebrows shot up to her hairline and her eyes rolled as she recalled her introduction to Esmé and hill farming, 'Peter had come with Esmé for company and, as we proceeded on the journey in the car, his knuckles turned white as he clung to the dashboard.'

Edna's first task the following morning was milking the cows, the three or four Highland cattle which Esmé believed suited the Welsh terrain and climate better than the Welsh Black cattle, but on that first day Edna was nonplussed.

'Those cattle were not milkers and they had so much hair it was difficult to locate the udder. "Come with me," Esmé said, and she gave me a not terribly clean bucket, took me down to the buildings the other side of the road and said, "Here's the cow, the milker, the one recently calved." There was no thought of washing the udder and when I had finished I went up to the house and said, "It's not very clean milk," Esmé gave me a crisp piece of muslin and I poured the milk through the filter and, thankfully, it went through. I really didn't know how to deal with dirty milk – after all, I'd done bacteriology. I soon lost all that and the upper-class!'

Edna is now a spry lady in her eighties. She still farms on her own near Beaumaris, Anglesey, and is full of energy.

'Esmé lived in bedlam, but she had given no real thought about hygiene. I remember shearing and sale days at Dyffryn. I learnt to shear with the old shears and then because of the influence of Godfrey Bowen, a man from New Zealand, she bought electric shears and I had to learn the technique all over again. Esmé made meals for anyone who helped at shearing and sale days, and I remember those... we made it in a bucket or a dustbin. Well, a relatively clean bin or a bucket, I cleaned and cleaned it – AND CLEANED IT – and then put the rice pudding in the bin on a Primus.'

Edna worked at Dyffryn for eight years and remained good friends with Esmé. She then married farmer David Jones of Gwastad Annas, who had been so kind to Esmé during the caravan years. He sold his hill farm and moved to a smaller holding on Anglesey. I asked Edna how she perceived the Esmé years – her answer was blunt:

'Oh, she was honest; she was willing to work because she had the right perspective on life. If you don't get up and bloody well get on with it, you don't deserve anything. She was great. Mind you, she was very cross when I got married.'

I looked at her and made the comment, 'Perhaps she didn't want you to leave.' Edna paused, 'She didn't admit that at the time, but eventually she confessed to me, "The gap of years between you and David was too much." And when she could see we were happy, we had a lovely daughter who is now a corporate lawyer in Dublin with two lovely little girls, in the end she told me that she had been wrong to make such a judgement.'

I asked Edna if Esmé was a good farmer. 'Well she was... She was not a natural animal person. She didn't have that feeling for animals like I've got or David my husband had. She did all the right things. But you know, if I go around the

fields, I'll hone in on something wrong. Esmé didn't do that
– she did everything that should be done but it wasn't in her
soul.'

* * *

The relationship between Peter and Esmé became closer
and, when Peter was demobilised after the war, he set up
a workshop in Dyffryn's old house and became a full-time
cabinet maker. They socialized at a newly-opened hotel a
mile or two up the road.

Pen-y-Gwryd Hotel began its life as a farmhouse in 1811.
In 1847 Henry Owen converted the building into a hotel,
with the intention of attracting interested mountaineers.
The business had mixed fortunes until the twentieth
century when new owners, Arthur and Florence Lockwood,
further developed the property and created a small trout
lake directly opposite the hotel, which they named Lake
Lockwood. During the Second World War the hotel was
taken over by Lake House School, Bexhill-on-Sea. In 1947
Chris and Jo Briggs became the new owners. The hotel
was refurbished, a mountain rescue post established and
mountaineering was again encouraged. Six years later it
received worldwide attention when it became known that
the 1953 Everest expedition had trained and tested oxygen
equipment there before setting forth on the successful epic
climb. Esmé and Peter joined the midnight champagne
celebrations there as news came through that the highest
peak in the world had been conquered. Today the success
of the 1953 team is remembered in the Everest room where
signed photographs, memorabilia and the unique report
written by James Morris for *The Times* on Coronation
Day provide a memory of the achievement. The hotel is

now run by the Briggs' two grandchildren, Rupert and Nick Pullee.

Chris and Jo became close friends with Esmé and Peter, and the Pen-y-Gwryd Hotel was a place to eat, meet people and relax. They also made good friends with many of those who visited or stayed at the hotel. Many of these would be invaluable to Esmé when she later established the Snowdonia National Park Society in 1967.

* * *

Tasks around the farm seemed endless and, for company and work, there were new friends: Glen, the sheepdog, had taken over from Luck and the rather elderly Turk, and Googie, a kid from the wild goat herd in the mountains, was reared by Esmé when its mother died. Googie became part of the family, going on many walks, two or three times a week, not for pleasure, but to check that the sheep and cattle were healthy.

Hot or humid days were perfect conditions for blow flies to attack sheep; the subsequent maggots ate flesh, creating deep sores in the skin. When a sheep rubbed fiercely against a pole or rock, it was a sure sign that maggots were on the attack and the sheep would soon lose condition unless treatment was started immediately, by shearing and cleaning the wool around the wound and clearing maggots. Other diseases included the dreaded foot-rot, one of the commonest in sheep, which was treated by trimming hooves and vaccination.

Constant vigilance was needed at lambing time, making it the most intense of all the tasks in the hill farmer's year. The revered Welsh poet, R.S. Thomas, had a living in mid Wales and then at Aberdaron in Llŷn. There he observed hill farmers going about their comfortless, lonely work, with little relief reflected on their faces in church on Sundays. In 'The Welsh Hill Country' he recalls:

> Too far for you to see
> The fluke and the foot-rot and the fat maggot
> Gnawing the skin from the small bones

However, there was no greater satisfaction than seeing the enclosed *ffridd* or a field becoming full of new life. The farmhouse was often home to a few lambs keeping warm in cardboard boxes, bottle-fed because the mother had died at birth or had rejected her lamb.

By now Esmé had lived and worked in the mountains for a decade and a half. In 1950 she wrote of her affection for the Glyderau in a publication compiled by her good friend Chris Brasher, *Portraits of Mountains*. This excerpt sums up her love for the landscape, and was read at her funeral:

> My portrait of the Glyders is bound to be a bit lopsided. Our house is perched on the western side of my farm, Dyffryn, takes in [over] 3,000 acres of summits and western slopes. The boundaries go along the highest point on the ridge between the Ogwen Valley, then down the side that overlooks the magnificent Llanberis Pass.
>
> The Glyders are the plain Janes of an incredibly good-looking family. Whatever way you look at them the Glyders are just a lump, a great rocky mass, an elongated many-humped camel's back, set right in the middle of all this mountain beauty. If not beauties themselves, they are a grand viewpoint for mountain scenery.
>
> But if you should go walking on them, and you get to know them as I do you will find that the Glyders, like so many plain people, have a charm, a personality, and a romantic interest all of their own.
>
> Heather, whin, tussocky *Molinia* grass, tumbled rocks and just enough mountain grass to give a living to about 3,000 sheep; that

39

is the Glyders. But mostly it is rock; there is hardly an acre in the eight square miles that is rock-free, great piles of boulders, great cliffs of glacier-scarred rocks. They rise, ridge upon ridge, until you reach that incredible climax on top of Glyder Fawr.

I do not know how many hundreds of sheep have lived in the Glyders. Our old farmhouse is over five hundred years old, and the farmer then was probably shepherding sheep on the Glyders in much the same way as we do today.

People often ask why our farmhouse is placed in such an inaccessible place, two hundred feet above the main road, perched up on the side of the mountain overlooking the Snowdon Valley. A steep track leading to it is our despair, for most of the one hundred and twenty inches of rain seems to take fiendish delight in continually washing away the surface.

I love the perched-up feeling of the house and would not change it for the world. I like the little belt of ragged windswept trees that surround it, the only trees on the whole of the Glyders. There is a new house now built right in front of the old one; she is a mere baby, not yet a hundred years old. The granite walls are eighteen inches thick but, in spite of them, the house trembles gently when there is a real Dyffryn gale blowing.

I suppose to an eye used to towns the Glyders did look a bit grim. I looked and saw beyond the mist. I saw the great ridge climbing from the Llanberis Pass, every outline clear against the winter sky. I looked at the great black crags immediately above me. I saw the sheep industriously nibbling away at the heather, and our mountain wall winding along the side, six miles long and six feet high. Every stone had to be carried for its building by some patient worker at Dyffryn before me.

Just after the war, the army came to repair some of the damage they had done during training. It was January, and a bitter east wind blew for a whole fortnight. The men toiled slowly and unwillingly, hating every moment of it. On the last day one of them said to me, 'Where's this mountain that that chap wrote a book about?' One sweep of my arm indicated the whole length of the Glyders, looking I admit, a little bleak, a little austere in the winter wind. His eye travelled slowly over the grey rocks and the dark heather from Capel to Cwm Ffynnon and back again. Then he turned away in disgust: 'What a dammed awful place to write a book about' was his only comment.

I thought of the exciting boulder-tossed summit of the Glyder Fach, of Castell y Gwynt, of the Cantelever Rock, of the Devil's Kitchen, that great cleft in the rocks just above Llyn Idwal. When the wind is blowing and the spray is whipped out of the cleft, 'the devil is brewing his tea' the old people used to say.

I remembered how I could walk on some part of them nearly all the year, and always find them looking different, never dull, never feeling I knew all there was to know. The best part if I had been away was swinging round the corner at Capel and seeing the Glyders.

Maybe I am biased. To me they are not just another mountain – the Glyders are, and always will be, my home.

5

THOMAS AND ESMÉ Firbank divorced in 1942. Thomas later married Tessa Coudret in 1943. He wrote in *I Bought a Star*, 'I no longer wanted to live my private life in the past which was buried in a Welsh mountain.' His second marriage produced two children, Louise, born in 1943, and Johanna, in 1946. Thomas had transferred ownership of the farm, house and cottages to Esmé and the dream of both of them living together happily forever was finally put to rest. And when Peter's divorce was finalised he married Esmé on 20 August 1949 at Conwy Valley Registry Office.

Peter had little interest in sheep farming but the mountain location of Dyffryn was perfect for him. He liked the outdoors, the landscape, the space, and the hostelries at both ends of the valley. Dyffryn was a remote and peaceful eyrie to refine his skills as a cabinet maker and to plan the refurbishment of the farmhouse. Peter and Esmé were well suited, but a few people maintained they were opposites. He, influenced by his years as a military man, preferred to plan in detail before taking action. She, however, was quick-thinking, making decisions that would leave those around her playing catch-up, but dealing daily with a large flock of sheep on difficult terrain had given her a modicum of patience.

* * *

Esmé worked hard to improve the quality of her flock but the margin of profit and loss was small when winters were particularly harsh. And the winter of 1947 was just that. It began snowing on 21 January and there was no sign of a thaw until mid-March. The heavy snowfall and wind for weeks on end caused severe snowdrifts, some twenty feet high. Within hours of the snow starting, the contours of the mountains changed, roads and railways became impassable. By mid-February the power stations began running out of coal, and the Government was forced to cut electricity for hours. Food supplies were in short supply.

The mountain sheep already enclosed in the *ffridd* lost weight, as it was almost impossible to get supplies of hay to them. Hundreds got caught in deep snowdrifts and perished; some froze to death where they stood sheltering against a wall or post. It was the same scene across the country and, when the thaw set in, the frozen ground caused severe flooding in the lowlands. It was the worst winter in living memory – estimates reported that a quarter of the sheep in Snowdonia had perished. Financially, it was catastrophic. The snow in the mountains did not clear completely until May and, as a result, the lambing season was poor – the pregnant ewes, although they'd been wintered on farms in the coastal lowlands, were weakened from weeks in freezing conditions. They had lost their bloom, not from neglect, but from the lack of finance to buy adequate feed due to the extended hard winter. This harsh winter meant that it took four to six difficult years to re-stock the flock.

The 1947 losses were severe but the country slowly recovered and, as the decade came to an end, austerity from war rationing eased too. The Labour party swept into power in the 1945 general election and immediately began a process of nationalising heavy industries such as coal and steel, and establishing the National Health Service in 1947. There was also much debate about nationalising

43

the land, but the government was preoccupied with other more pressing reforms. That same year, legislation was passed which provided farmers with a degree of security and prosperity, including regulated markets, guaranteed prices and an annual price review – a huge step forward in economic planning. For hill farmers attempting to recover from the severe losses of 1947, it was welcome news. It would avoid another slump, but during the 1950s agriculture became driven by subsidies, market forces and environmental considerations, all three assuming greater importance.

* * *

Tourism flourished in Snowdonia, with more and more people enjoying the great outdoors. The numbers visiting Snowdonia for pleasure rose rapidly. Local communities and authorities began to fear that developers would move in to cash in on this. Caravan parks proliferated on land near the coastal areas, with little thought towards design or landscaping. After the war these caravans provided cheap accommodation for thousands of people who longed to spend their two-week holiday in the open air by the sea. Daytrips to see the dramatic landscape of Snowdonia by car, bus or train became desirable and easier, and the pressure on facilities grew. There was the belief that an 'open mountain' was an open invitation to walk anywhere.

Billy Butlin, the holiday camp entrepreneur, had realised the potential of the north Wales coastline even before the outbreak of the Second World War. He had bought a tract of land near Pwllheli and agreed a secret deal to build an admiralty training camp which, at the end of the war, would be used as a holiday camp. When this plan was discovered at the end of the war, local planners were horrified, and sustained opposition came from many who were concerned with the imposition of a mass urbanised culture on the Welsh-speaking heartland of the Llŷn peninsula. Billy Butlin got approval, and his holiday camp was opened in 1947 and continues to this day.

Snowdonia was certainly beginning to feel the pressure from the influx of summer tourists. Local farmers, informed visitors, walkers, climbers, politicians and environmentalists began debating about the future of this beautiful area. Two hundred years earlier the poet Wordsworth had claimed that the similar landscape of the Lake District was 'untamed countryside', a kind of national property, in which 'every man has a right and interest who has an eye to perceive and a heart to enjoy'. The first Freedom to Roam Bill was introduced to Parliament in 1884. It was defeated, as were ten other attempts until 2000 when the Countryside and Rights of Way Act was passed and gave the public conditional rights to walk in certain areas of England and Wales, such as moorland, heathland and coastal land.

Esmé had always treasured the landscape around her farm and had herself tried various schemes to provide facilities for tourists. However, the need to protect the environment from misuse became an urgent concern of hers, too.

One such example was when the British Electricity Authority declared its intention in the late 1940s to create huge reservoirs in a few of the local valleys: Nant Gwynant, Nant Ffrancon, Cwm Croesor, Crafnant and Cwm Penamnen. The electricity generated there would supply the new National Grid, and the reservoirs, in turn, would boost tourism by providing excellent opportunities for sailing and fishing. Pressure against this plan was shown from the local community, together with many groups and societies, and the British Electricity Authority would have gone ahead with their plan but for the voice of an experienced Welsh parliamentarian. Megan Lloyd George MP, raised the proposal in Parliament in 1950 and argued that such a strategy did not make sense in an area that was about to be designated a National Park.

Establishing National Parks in 1951 was meant to enhance the areas' natural beauty and provide recreational opportunities for the public. Other parts of the world had long since established parks – Yellowstone in the USA was the first in 1872 and Sweden had established nine in 1909. The first National Park to be declared in Britain was the Peak District in 1951, followed by the Lake District, and Snowdonia later that year. The following became National Parks within the next decade: Dartmoor, Pembrokeshire Coast, North Yorkshire Moors, Yorkshire Dales, Exmoor, Northumberland and Brecon Beacons.

Clough Williams-Ellis, the architect of Portmeirion, the Italianate village near Penrhyndeudraeth, was a tireless campaigner for the environment. In 1928 he became a founder member and the first chairman of the Council for the Preservation of Rural Wales (CPRW). He was an influential advocate of National Parks, and it was he who was responsible for demarcating the boundary of Snowdonia National Park. It turned out to be the second-largest National Park in the UK, totalling 857 square miles including thirty-seven miles of coastline.

The National Parks Commission, the overall ruling body for the parks in the early years, set up an independent board to manage the Peak District and the Lake District National Parks. The other eight Parks, including Snowdonia, would to be managed by boards run by local county councils. The proposed area of Snowdonia National Park encompassed three separate county councils: Caernarfon, Meirionnydd and Denbigh – a planning nightmare causing immense difficulties. Months of argument between these authorities failed to settle on a constitution for the Snowdonia National Park Board, so the next option was to form a committee, a joint advisory committee (a very Welsh compromise), but at least this decision was a stimulus for work to begin. It was 1953 by now, and two long years since the Snowdonia National Park had been designated.

Esmé took a keen interest in the establishment of the Snowdonia National Park and its governance. She was concerned it would affect the landscape and the farming communities living within its boundaries. She became interested in the decisions of the Park's advisory committee and her voice could often be heard at meetings, especially where planning matters regarding industrial buildings, roads and footpaths were discussed. These were of concern to many local people too. Esmé was a confident speaker and her opinions became more passionate and forceful as the years passed. She was a conservationist, an ardent defender of the mountain landscape, and she was convinced it should remain as it was without any major commercial development. She wasn't against progress, but the landscape within the Park should be kept unspoilt.

Clough's sister-in-law, Cecily Williams-Ellis, already an activist in many controversial environmental planning issues, had established the Caernarfon branch of the CPRW in 1928. When the joint advisory committee for Snowdonia National Park was established in 1953, she was invited to be one of its original members. The CPRW was a highly-respected consultation body for national and local government and, together with other environmental and heritage groups, they were often asked to undertake the necessary lobbying campaigns. Esmé knew Cecily to be a knowledgeable campaigner, and knew how thorough and tenacious she could be.

Cecily had arrived in Eifionydd following her marriage to Rupert Williams-Ellis, the heir to the Glasfryn Estate near Pwllheli. She was twenty-three and he was forty-five; and three sons were born to the couple at the ancestral home. Her family, the Hambro banking family, had disapproved of her marriage but she created a good life at Glasfryn, immersing herself in the history of the estate and the area and, without doubt, she became a passionate, active, respected and influential lobbyist for many years. When Rupert died Cecily moved to Tŷ Nanney, Porthmadog, and continued to live there for forty years, working tirelessly as chair of the Caernarfon branch of the CPRW.

* * *

The main pressure in the formative years of the Park, especially for those living and working on the land, was the increasing numbers who came to walk on inadequate paths. This meant that surrounding areas were destroyed, with the landscape they'd come to enjoy disappearing. Goronwy Roberts, the Caernarfon MP, expressed his own fears when he suggested that the purpose of a national park was to establish some kind of 'Indian Reserve'.

As a result the Snowdonia National Park received a mixed welcome from the local community. Its first campaign was to educate the public to respect the countryside – to keep to the paths, to close gates and not disturb crops, farm animals or wildlife. With cooperation from other agencies over a period of years, it set out to promote the Countryside Code, a practice that still continues today.

Another early aim of the Park was to alleviate pressures and problems for visitors in popular areas by providing car parks and establishing information centres. The first of the latter was opened in Llanrwst, and the second in Dolgellau in 1959.

However other more serious developments were beyond the Park's control, such as tree planting by the Forestry Commission; the controversial 1957 Act passed to build a nuclear power station at Trawsfynydd; and the 1957 Bill passed permitting Liverpool Corporation to drown the Tryweryn Valley in Meirionnydd, despite every Welsh MP voting against the proposal. Eight hundred acres were lost to the reservoir: twelve farms, a village community including a school, post office and chapel disappeared under the water. During the following years, as the dam was being built, there were national protests and serious unrest at Liverpool Corporation's apathy in ignoring the general consensus of Welsh opinion. Eight years later, on 25 October 1965, Llyn Celyn was officially opened, becoming the biggest dam in Wales. As the historian Dr John Davies wrote in *History of Wales*, 'Liverpool's ability to ignore the virtually unanimous opinion of the representatives of the Welsh people confirmed one of the central tenets of Plaid Cymru – that the national Welsh community, under the existing order, was wholly powerless.'

Closer to home, Esmé and Peter saw change at the Royal Hotel, Capel Curig, in 1955. It became Plas y Brenin, a national mountain sports centre (these days under the aegis of Sport England), and a memorial to the late King George VI. The centre provided residential training facilities for climbing, as well as kayaking, canoeing and sailing on

Llynnau Mymbyr and Cardigan Bay nearby. It also catered for the Duke of Edinburgh Awards. In many respects the area was already being used for such sporting activities – Peter had been in command of Sandhurst's battle camp nearby, providing outdoor education courses for young soldiers.

Such developments drew attention to the area, its landscape and beauty, and naturally tourists were drawn to visit in increasing numbers too. Esmé became a member of CPRW, but not a committee member. She consistently made her concerns known about the amount of litter left in lay-bys, the need to provide adequate viewing points at strategic places, and the need to create detailed maps showing footpaths, and coordinate efforts and finance to maintain them. Esmé was frustrated that action by the relevant agencies and authorities on these matters was so slow, and that there was a growing tension between the interests of local communities and the tourists who came to enjoy the landscape.

Another concern was the proposed nuclear power station being built near Trawsfynydd, a menacing concrete construction project within the heart of the beautiful national park. It was designed by the distinguished architect, Sir Basil Spence. The construction work did provide employment in an area where there was a serious lack of job opportunities, especially for skilled workers. But not only were there concerns about the visual impact, the thought of possible leakage from the plant seemed uppermost in the minds of those who lived in the area.

And when the plant was officially opened, the community then became worried about the consequences after the plant ceased production. Waste material, a dump of nuclear material the size of two football pitches, would be kept within the building for at least another forty years. A statement made in a public inquiry provoked further worry the prospect of one hundred years or more of nuclear storage in a national park was disgraceful, a nightmare.

But for Esmé the pressures on the Snowdonia terrain were more immediate. She would put her case to various councils, authorities, agencies and influential individuals, her manner always passionate and persistent. A Welsh Office minister nominated her to be a member of the National Park advisory committee, but she found that experience uncomfortable as the majority of the committee members were representative of three county councils.

She would explore her views, thoughts and ideas about the future of the Snowdonia landscape with Peter. Their debates apparently were heated, but without rancour; she respected his views which were voiced quietly and firmly. One or two close friends believed that Peter always gave in to her way of thinking. But, rather, he was actually helping her construct an effective argument when she spoke at public meetings. She wrote letters to the press, she counselled her favourite journalists with her opinions. She was working her way to being centre stage.

6

IT WAS BECOMING crystal clear to Esmé that Snowdonia National Park needed some kind of a watchdog, an independent voluntary body which would question decisions by the advisory committee on matters such as road planning, forestry policies, industrial development, access, car parking, creating pathways, use of natural materials in buildings, and so on. Esmé was the first to voice her opinion on this matter in public. She'd already had discussions about this with like-minded friends in a series of meetings at Dyffryn. The watchdog she proposed would not be a talking shop but an 'action' society.

In describing the role of a watchdog, she wrote, 'That we will remain for all time not a walkers' society or a farmers' society, neither a Welsh nor an English society – a society for all who care for the Snowdonia National Park.'

A public meeting was convened at Betws-y-coed on 10 June 1967 with 127 people attending. After a question and answer session, it was resolved to formalise ideas and constitute the Snowdonia National Park Society, with Esmé as its chair. There were a few dissenting voices, with some feeling that the CPRW was an organisation active in these matters, but Esmé felt that the CPRW was too conservative and too cautious. She had already, apparently, crossed swords with the influential Cecily Williams-Ellis, the chair of the Caernarfon branch of CPRW, who researched her campaigns thoroughly and was an effective leader. No-one can explain what prompted the two women's disagreement, but their feud was well known and deep-seated and, as Esmé was concerned, she decided to start her own society. And in June 1967, she did just that.

The advisory committee responsible for the running of Snowdonia National Park welcomed the concept of a watchdog (the Peak District National Park already had such a body), and it hoped for a healthy and constructive working relationship with its watchdog. Both bodies, naturally, had the well-being of the Park at heart. Fourteen members were elected to the committee of the Snowdonia National Park Society, and officers were selected including chair, secretary and treasurer and they set to work immediately. The Society held ten meetings from July 1967 to October 1968.

At the inaugural meeting in July, the committee was informed that the Gorffwysfa Hotel at Pen-y-Pass was being purchased by the Youth Hostel Association. This caused a heated debate within the Society, especially by those (led by Esmé) who felt that the general public locally was being deprived of an important facility if the historic hotel closed. Others felt strongly that a youth hostel run by a major provider of cheap accommodation was an asset and a considerable force in educating youngsters and others about the appropriate use of the countryside. The arguments continued at several further meetings, but eventually the committee felt that a 'change of use was borderline' – it was not a cause to pursue any further. But the question of needing a car park at Pen-y-Pass for the ever-increasing visitors was essential, and the Society would be keeping a watching brief on developments.

Other on-going concerns included the amount of litter which had reached an all-time high that summer. The Society's first annual report written by Esmé for 1968 records: 'We are against constantly asking our members to clean up after a dirty public unless it involves constructive action. Nor do we believe that more and more litter bins are the answer – litter begets litter.' A heading for the next paragraph states, 'Litter control experiment in Snowdon Valley'. The report continues, 'On 28 August, four lay-bys between Capel Curig and Pen-y-Gwryd were cleared. Collection from one lay-by was: 29 milk bottles, 41 assorted bottles, 111 tins and 2,143 pieces of paper and torn cardboard. We had no idea that the great British public was so addicted to tea bags!'

Another cause of discontent for the Society was, 'The increasing tension between those who work in the mountains – the hill farmers – and those who come to enjoy them.' Farmers on the Glyderau had experienced so many broken walls and fences that they had closed parts of their farms to the public.

Members of the Society's committee met farmers to discuss concerns and to see what help they could offer. The farming community agreed to allow the Society to mark routes and put up stiles and notices in a few places on the Glyderau mountains. The annual report states: 'The Plas y Brenin warden, John A. Jackson, was so pleased with the proposal that he offered to make the stiles. The offer was gratefully accepted. It took a long time working out routes and selecting the most suitable stiles – it might interest members that five methods of lettering for small neat signs, and about twenty shades of green were considered before a decision was taken, and only time will show whether we made the right decision.'

But when the stiles were finished they were so heavy that it was impossible to carry them up the Glyderau, so the RAF was asked to help. On Friday, 1 November 1968, Operation Stiles took place, and an RAF helicopter from the Central Flying School, Valley, Anglesey, landed at Plas y Brenin and made three trips to the mountains and, in a matter of minutes, the stiles were in place. The report continues, 'We hope the path will be open to the public in two or three weeks' time. It will go over the two mountains, Glyder Fach and Glyder Fawr from Capel Curig to Pen-y-Pass, and will be the great ridge walk of Britain. If this is successful we hope that we may be able to help other farmers who have similar problems; it must be stressed that these routes do not constitute public footpaths, they are on private land.' (In 1973 Esmé would have good news to report. The Society had won a Prince of Wales award for the courtesy paths on the Glyderau, an appreciation for the Society's hard work.)

This first annual report ended with a plea for subscriptions. 'As we become more active our expenses will increase considerably. The committee tries to save every administrative penny. There is this point too. A Society with a large membership can be powerful and influential. So, will you not only pay your sub, but try and enrol another member.' It seems it was already a Society in 'action', but the chair, however enthusiastic and determined, failed to get her way with every campaign.

A former experienced chair of the CPRW, Elizabeth Colwyn-Foulkes, who knew Esmé and saw her at work, gave this observation, 'Esmé wasn't what I would call a team person or a committee member. She was a stand-alone figure that you got behind and supported her campaigns. She was a charismatic figure, she had so much passion, an attractive looking person and personality, and when she had a hobbyhorse and a cause, she found people to support her.'

Caerwyn Roberts, chair of the Snowdonia National Park Authority gives another view of Esmé in committee action. 'When she walked towards you at a committee meeting you knew at once what mood she was in. If she bit her lips into a straight line it was not good, you could feel the tension inside her. I remember once her comment, her lips straighter than usual when she said, "Unless we're careful the whole of Snowdonia will be under bricks and mortar." I smiled and I said, "Well as long as I'm here Esmé I'll try my best to incorporate stone into it." She looked at me, paused, and began to smile, and put her two hands on my shoulders and whispered, "Good Boy." Once she had crystallised her point of view, you had to be a very special person to change it. She was like a little terrier, once she had bitten, she would not let go.'

David Firth, who took over the Snowdonia National Park Society's chairmanship from Esmé very many years later, added: 'Esmé created the Society which was a brilliant concept. She also gave us financial backing in a very short time compared with other national park societies. We were up and running and our finances were on a sure footing. She made sure she went for every penny she could, and it went straight into the bank. In the initial years, when the headquarters were at Dyffryn, she spent very little on administration. She loved to see money going into the bank and was very reluctant to see anything spent.'

With the Society well and truly launched, Esmé took a hard look at her lifestyle. Now approaching her sixties, farming was still taking much of her time and energy. The Society was demanding: there were committees to attend, events in the National Park to visit, lobbying influential leaders in the countryside was needed, getting to grips with increasing the membership and keeping them informed, and so on. With Society paperwork mounting and the demands on a hands-on farmer constant, Esmé was torn between the two. She wanted to remain a farmer – it was her living and she could not consider leaving Dyffryn but, on the other hand, she aspired to develop the Snowdonia National Park Society into an effective and respected body.

She wrestled with the dilemma for quite some time until she found a solution. She decided to make Will, the shepherd and her right hand man, the manager. She would also advertise for another pair of hands. This decision was a load off her shoulders as she knew that Will was skilled and knowledgeable. More important, she could trust the loyal shepherd.

* * *

The National Parks Commission was replaced by the Countryside Commission in 1968. It proved to be a stronger organisation, with finance to employ more staff and encourage innovative schemes.

One three-year project taken up by the Snowdonia National Park and supported by the Countryside Commission was an upland management scheme which dealt with access to the countryside on the Rhinogydd range which includes Rhinog Fawr, Rhinog Fach, and Llethr, at 2,481 feet, which is near Cadair ldris. This isolated area was popular with hill walkers, with varying terrain: rocky and heather-clad to the north at Harlech and grassier to the south overlooking the Mawddach estuary. There were not many designated footpaths in this area and, once again with farmers' cooperation, the situation was improved by creating a network of paths, stiles and signposts and small car parks.

Another issue for the Park was a request from the Welsh Scout Council to develop an outdoor pursuits' centre and camping site at Cornel Farm, near the shore of Llyn Crafnant. Many people strongly objected to the development, as the lake had been designated a reservoir in 1874 to supply water to Llanrwst and Trefriw in the Conwy Valley. Local councils, organisations and agencies joined together to oppose the scheme, but the Welsh Office minister supported the application and planning permission was granted.

Mynydd Deulyn (Mountain of Two Lakes) separated Llyn Crafnant from Llyn Geirionydd on the slopes of the Carneddau range on the northern side of the Gwydyr Forest. A well-researched objection to water-skiing and other mechanised sports on Llyn Geirionydd, a natural lake, was turned down by Caernarfon County Council, much to the dismay of local residents. Llyn Geirionydd is the only lake to have a permit for motor boats and water-skiing – objections to the noise have regularly been presented to the Welsh Office since, but each one has been turned down.

7

A s the new decade dawned, 1970 was designated the European Conservation Year. In October a 'Countryside in 1970' conference received reports from interested working groups: subjects covered the use of derelict land, refuse, research and professional services, education and information, ethics and youth. But the main thrust of the conference was discussing the implications of urbanisation, industry, agriculture, forestry and leisure pursuits in the countryside.

It certainly seemed that the industrialisation of Snowdonia was marching on. Apart from the nuclear plant at Trawsfynydd and the dam at Tryweryn, two other major industrial companies wanted to become part of the Park.

Rio Tinto Zinc, a large British mining company, had applied to explore for copper in Meirionnydd, and to dredge for gold in the Mawddach estuary. Snowdonia is littered with the debris of mineralization: ores of copper, lead, zinc, iron, gold; and traces of mines, mill buildings, wheel-pits, water leats and transport systems from a bygone age. News of Rio Tinto Zinc's intention galvanised almost every authority and public body to campaign against the scheme. However, as the result of a public inquiry, the Secretary of State for Wales granted permission for one year's exploratory drilling. The campaigning continued, but should the drilling be successful, open-cast mining for copper would begin. The 1973 Snowdonia National Park Society annual report records, 'After all the publicity and concern over Rio Tinto's mining activities, it was strange that their decision to withdraw from the Park passed almost without notice.' But Esmé, with due diligence, added that open-cast mining was not an attractive commercial proposition at that time. 'Mind you, if the price of copper rises they will look again at the Park... The price of beauty is eternal vigilance... and action.'

The other major industrial proposal was building the Dinorwig Power Station pump storage scheme. Storing energy here meant that the plant could release electricity when consumers' needs surged. A lake above Llanberis, Marchlyn Mawr, was to be enlarged into a dam to release a head of water, when needed, into the generators down below at the power station. The whole costly building scheme turned the Elidir Fawr mountain into an enormous shell – gouging the body and soul out from inside the mountain, as millions of tonnes of rock were removed to create a huge internal cavern and tunnels. Lorries used newly-created roads to dump their loads elsewhere, and conservationists wondered how much defacement would remain when the construction work had finished.

During work to create one of these new roads, Esmé's phone rang to say that a fleet of lorries were dumping tonnes of slate waste to build a road along the bank of Llyn Peris. Esmé drove immediately to the site to see that a hole had been made in a boundary. 'Does the owner have permission?' she asked a workman and he replied, 'Don't think so, but you can usually get away with it if you work fast enough.'

'Ridiculous' was Esmé's riposte, but as she wrote in the Society's annual report, an enforcement order could not be served unless authorised by the main Snowdonia Park Committee which only met every three or four months. The enforcement officer had apparently been there, but the owner had taken no notice and carried on. Indeed the completed road could have had time to develop potholes before an enforcement order could have been served on the owner.

Esmé wrote: 'We were nonplussed... It was some of our Gwynant members who saved the day (and the defacement of the lakeside) and kept the Society flag flying in splendid style.' Tom Kinsey, a member of the committee, was a resourceful man. No-one could stop him parking his car on the roadside in front of the hole to 'admire the view'. A second fleet of lorries arrived. They begged, they pleaded, but Tom sat firm. The driver of the bulldozer was about to put his hand on a lever when Chris Brasher then arrived in his new and expensive sports car and blocked the other half of the opening. The vigil continued all day and the next, but by late afternoon on the third day the contractors had had enough. They left. That was a typical example of the enthusiasm, determination and concern of members of the watchdog society.

Chris Brasher was a distinguished journalist, broadcaster and sports editor who had taken a prominent part in the historic race at Iffley Road Stadium, Oxford, in 1954 – the first sub-four minute mile race, which was won by Roger Bannister. Two years later, in Melbourne, he won the Olympic gold medal for the 3,000-metre steeplechase and, together with another Olympic bronze medallist steeplechaser, John Disley, they pioneered the sport of orienteering in the mountains. Later, in 1981, they established the London Marathon. They worked together on a commercial venture, the Sweatshop and the South Navigation Club and in 1978, designed the Brasher Boot, a walking boot with the comfort of a running shoe. Both loved the mountains, both bought cottages in Snowdonia and became active in the Society. John is president of the Society today, but Chris passed away in 2003. He is still remembered for his vision and principles and, as a mourner at his funeral said of him, 'Chris was one of those rare individuals who could make things happen. He had the most amazing drive and vision.'

* * *

The most significant change in the governance of the Snowdonia National Park came with the 1974 reorganisation of local government in Wales. The three councils, Caernarfon, Meirionnydd and Anglesey were merged into one, Gwynedd, the familiar title of one of the medieval kingdoms of Wales. Clough Williams-Ellis must have had the kingdom of Gwynedd in mind when he proposed the boundaries of the Snowdonia National Park. When Gwynedd County Council was established it was appropriate to form one central authority to govern the Park. Thus, administration became easier, giving the Park the ability to attract financial backing for new schemes and to create a unified vision. In addition, the Park now assumed responsibility for planning, but applications outside the defined Park boundaries were handled by Gwynedd County Council.

The first major investment of this new era was the opening of an acquisition made five years earlier, Plas Tan y Bwlch, near Maentwrog. This country house had been extensively renovated and refurbished to become a study centre for those interested in all aspects of the countryside, be it geological, botanical or historical. The imposing estate overlooking the River Dwyryd had been the home of the Oakley family between 1789 and 1961. The lucrative local slate industry, including the largest subterranean quarry in the world, had brought prosperity and great wealth to landowners such as the Oakleys. And today the estate is a considerable asset for the Park, providing accommodation for meetings and conferences.

Despite the changes being made in the future in the administration and governance of the Park, Esmé didn't take her eye off-the-ball; neither did members of the Society. One morning in December 1973 the secretary of the Society, Harvey Lloyd, was driving his children from Pen-y-Pass Youth Hostel where he was the joint manager, to catch the school bus in Nant Peris. He'd seen workmen widening the A4086, and soon they would reach the Cromlech Boulders and the old stone bridge. He dropped the girls at the bus stop and, on the return journey, saw traffic lights in operation – the road was a yard and a half wider by now and heading straight for the boulders. He also saw that a sizeable lump was already missing from one boulder. These Cromlech Boulders had become part of local folklore from times long forgotten. Tales were told of giants and fairies living under them; Hetty, an eighteenth-century character had made her home there, and Joe Brown, the legendary climber, used to sleep under them.

A few days later Harvey Lloyd spotted two men with pneumatic drills standing on the boulders, already drilling holes to be filled with explosives. With swiftness of mind he stopped the car and told them there was a huge row going on in the council offices in Caernarfon, and that there had been a change of mind in the highways' department, and they were to stop drilling until the county surveyor came to the site. With that he raced to the car and raced even faster to find a telephone. The first person he called was Esmé. She phoned the Park head office and many of her influential contacts. Harvey Lloyd was asked to phone Plas y Brenin and other associations and organisations, urging them to lobby the County Council. When he returned the workmen had left the site. Harvey parked his car under the first boulder. The media eventually got wind of the story and Lord Hunt (of Everest fame), at the time in the House of Lords, sent a telegram protesting firmly against the scheme.

Esmé, in typical fearless fashion, later said, 'It might be stretching a point to say that there was an international outcry, but climbers, historians, conservationists, geologists and the ordinary people who loved the Pass rallied to the defence of these great rocks.'

But there were others, local and vocal, who believed that the protest was against progress and organised by incomers to the area – an argument that became familiar in the years to come at other popular tourist areas. It took six years to resolve the boulders' issue and, at every move and turn, for and against – involving the County Council, the Park Authority, the Welsh Office and the Secretary of State, Peter Thomas – it was all reported in the media with headlines such as, 'The Explosive Battle of the Boulders' and 'Three Thousand Tons of Sentiment'. The diligent county surveyor eventually resolved the predicament and, by taking an inch here and a yard there, he managed to widen the road to his satisfaction – avoiding the Cromlech Boulders – leaving them where they had settled thousands of years earlier.

The Welsh Office and County Council highways departments were often deplored for their 'so-called improvements', in particular, the size, design and landscaping of roads in Snowdonia. But the Park Authority did not have the power to press for greater control. Esmé had read the hundred-foolscap-page plan, the 'monumental document' as she called it, of the Park Authority, entitled 'Snowdon and You', submitted in 1973 to the Government. Esmé orchestrated comments from the Society which were welcomed, but the final draft of the plan turned out to be a rather weak and negative document. For example, it did not make the case for the right to have control on important issues. Many members of the Park Authority were of the opinion that it would not be able to 'carry out its fundamental duty – to preserve, protect, cherish and enhance the superbly beautiful National Park'.

Another issue which exercised the Society was a two-mile stretch of road being built by the Central Electricity Generating Board (CEGB) across the Carneddau. One Society member called it, 'one of the most breathtaking pieces of vandalism I have ever seen'. In one of the most unspoilt areas of the Park, the road had bulldozed straight up the mountainside from the A5 to Ffynnon Llugwy. No attempt had been made to conceal it or to make it blend in with the mountain environment. Esmé had written directly to the Secretary of State for Wales, as the road did not comply with Section 49 of the 1973 North Wales Power Bill, that the CEGB should have regard to the preservation of the natural beauty of the district for the public. The Bill also stated that the CEGB's proposals should be placed before the planning authority and/or the Countryside Commission.

Esmé wrote in the Society's annual report in 1975, 'It seems that a grave breach of statutory procedure has occurred, some aspects have been ignored... We have said many times that we are not interested in allocating blame. We believe a mistake has been made and it should be rectified. We are resolutely determined that this outrageous scar on the Carneddau shall not be permanent.'

* * *

Esmé indeed won a few battles, but lost others. I asked John Disley, the current president of the Snowdonia Society, whether she was a bad loser? 'Well yes, she bore grudges gratefully – she gave that as the reason for arguing the next time, I think. I don't want to sound hard on her. I used to go skiing with her in Kitzbühel every February; the climbing club in the valley would arrange the trip. Esmé and I were the best skiers in the group, so we would set out at the crack of dawn because if there was one thing that upset her was standing in a queue. Then she'd set off – set a line – and I thought, I don't want to get killed as well – just stop, and watch it!'

But her husband Peter was not a natural skier and he always worked a cunning plan to avoid steep snow. The first day was the so-called 'settling in day': sharpening the skis and a *schnapps* or two. Any repairs would be left for day two, which would need a light lunch at a comfortable tavern, so that by the time he thought of skiing, the light would be fading. On day three he'd visit the local wood yard because it was useful for his cabinet-making interests. Day four could be exchanged for others in the week – and on day five he would take a lift up the mountain and join the others at the *Gasthaus* and would end up making the rounds of the best watering holes in the town. A real party – Peter never missed!

The domestic scene at Dyffryn dinner parties were occasions of formality, yet conviviality. Sylvia Disley recalled, 'Peter would ensure the wine was at the right temperature and Esmé would whiz around her kitchen, cooking at speed a delicious meal. The table was immaculately laid and then Peter would produce his 'swagger stick', a kind of measuring stick used by the military to place every piece of cutlery and glass in its place accurately, with serviettes folded precisely.'

Gunna Chown who, with her husband Chris, now runs

Plas Bodegroes Hotel, was at one time a secretary to Esmé at Dyffryn. 'Yes, two or three days a week. I started with her at lambing time. She had a little office and a sitting room. In front of the fire, there was a tiny little table, a typewriter, and a ghastly Roneo duplicator, plus little lambs in cardboard boxes all around the room. She would be in waterproofs and filthy; she'd come in smelling to high heaven, dictate ten letters and then look carefully at ewes about to give birth. At other times we would have a whole day in the office and when I left she would get into this huge lorry and take her sheep to Rhyl and, if it was autumn, to the place where they would winter at another farm. And she had already done a day's work... And she wasn't young then.'

David Firth had met Esmé for the first time in 1974 when he came to work at the Plas y Brenin outdoor education centre. At a Park committee meeting in Beddgelert, she invited him to Dyffryn to give him an outline of the Snowdonia National Park Society's affairs. 'We stood in the kitchen, and it was a turning point. I hadn't realised the amount of work needed to protect the environment, and it was really meeting her that changed my attitude. A lady totally in command.' And when he was asked, 'Was she frugal?' he replied, 'Oh yes, totally. Totally. Look at the cars she drove. They were old and always breaking down. About the only thing I can remember, if Esmé spent any money, was when she spent for special occasions. She would splash out on very nice outfits. But the house, she didn't really spend anything on. It was comfortable, but the kitchen was always in a mess.'

And that was the general opinion of everyone who visited Dyffryn; however she could cook marvellous food. Gunna Chown gave these observations. 'No hygiene, no tidiness, a complete mess in the kitchen, you couldn't find space and out of this came fantastic and delicious meals. I don't think she looked at a recipe book. When she went out to dinner she was so glamorous. Always, always made up, and always dyed her hair, right to the end and very attractive. She was always very smart.'

'A lot of an actress in her?'

'Very much so. Tough as nails, mind. She was a remarkable woman, driven. She really was. I'm glad I knew her.'

Peter had already carved a successful business at his workshop at Dyffryn and, with the sense of permanence that the marriage gave him, and his military background, he joined the Royal Welch Fusiliers Territorial Army. They invited him to design the layout for a new regimental museum in the Queen's Tower at Caernarfon Castle which was in a derelict state at the time: three floors, no staircases, no windows and broken stonework. When his plans for a renovation were accepted he began making display cabinets for the regiment's memorabilia: medals, uniforms, letters, citations and also a handsome wooden stairs between the floors within the tower. Richard Prichard, a retired museum assistant, told me with pride, 'You can tell he was a real craftsman, not one metal bolt. Nothing worried Major Kirby. He was the last of the old gentlemen of the army. He'd had far harder times than working in museums.'

Peter's knowledge of military matters and his craftsmanship was much admired and he was appointed curator and trustee in time for the opening of the museum in 1963. In the next few years he became a member of such august bodies as the court of governors of the National Museum of Wales and the National Library of Wales. As a craftsman he was invited to design and make chairs for the winning bards at two National Eisteddfodau – he was now accepted in a way that Esmé never quite managed; Peter was an integral part of Welsh culture and heritage.

He had also established a small library of books about military campaigns, such as Robert Graves's memories in *Goodbye to All That,* Siegfried Sassoon's *Memoirs of an Infantry Officer* and *In Parenthesis* by David Jones. There were regimental and battalion histories too on the shelves, and four books dealing with aspects of the regiment written by Major Kirby himself. His own *magnum opus* was *The Officers of the Royal Welch Fusiliers,* giving biographical notes on every officer of the regiment from its founding in 1689.

In terms of prominent Royal Welch Fusiliers, the poet Ellis Humphrey Evans is to this day honoured and revered in Wales. He submitted an ode for the chair at the National Eisteddfod held in Birkenhead in August 1917. Ellis was an unmarried poet, who lived with his family at Yr Ysgwrn, Trawsfynydd; he was also an unwilling member of the army. He wrote his poem, 'Yr Arwr' [The Hero] while on leave in the spring of 1917. When he returned to duty in Belgium, he was soon involved in one of the bloodiest battles of the First World War, the Battle of Passchendaele, near Ypres.

Every poet is required to use a nom de plume in competition and when the fleur-de-lis was called to the audience in the packed pavilion at Birkenhead, no-one stood to claim the chair. The archdruid then announced that 'Hedd Wyn' (Ellis Evans's bardic name) had won and that he'd been killed six weeks earlier on the fields of Flanders. In deep silence the chair was covered with a black cloth. The life story of Hedd Wyn was made into a film in 1992 and that was subsequently nominated for an Oscar. Today a statue stands to his memory at Trawsfynydd.

* * *

In the early 1970s, an appeal was made to increase the Society's membership, especially among people who could undertake voluntary work. Two hundred joined in 1975 and, at the end of 1976, a further three hundred had enrolled. Esmé wrote in that year's report: 'This is satisfactory but by no means a laurel-resting effort. Our target is a thousand members by the end of next year. It is a tough assignment but with the help of so many enthusiastic friends amongst our members, it may be possible.' Two hundred new members enrolled in 1977.

This was a decade when a number of themes appeared regularly in the annual reports; although how the Society tackled individual incidents depended on many factors. Every mound of litter had a peculiar history of its own; proposals by the Forestry Commission to plant new acres of spruce would mean the life of mature trees would be cut short. These were issues which exercised the Society. So, Esmé was in top gear writing letters of protest to council highway planners who wanted road widening schemes or had dreams of featureless straight roads through the beautiful Snowdonia countryside. She ended the 1975 annual report with an exhortation:

The Goal

Conservation is a state of harmony between man and land
– it sounds so simple and the idea has been around for a long time, but progress towards this goal is pitifully slow. Land is regarded as a commodity to be grabbed and exploited, but no people own the land. Title deeds may go back to the Doomsday Book but those who own land are only life tenants. They cannot take it with them as they can their money if they retreat to the Bahamas. They must leave the land behind. They have completed their tenancy. It can be covered with concrete, smothered with high-rise buildings, burnt or sold, but it cannot be destroyed.

National Parks are tiny remnants of our island where we may

hope to achieve this state of harmony. As long as we regard the land as something to be exploited, our Parks will be constantly under threat. We must think of them as great national treasures of incalculable value, to be lovingly cherished and respected and handed on unspoilt to the next generation. If we can do this, we may be starting to achieve that harmony. Only then can we be proud of our stewardship.

* * *

By the second half of the 1970s, the Sherpa bus service, an imaginative and practical scheme financed by the Countryside Commission, was in full swing transporting tourists and local people. It certainly helped ease traffic congestion in the Snowdon area. Esmé records, 'We have sent what we hope will be considered constructive suggestions to our National Park officer, for instance, the siting, design and colour of signs have had some adverse comments.'

Adverse comments did not cease either about the continuation of water-skiing on Llyn Geirionydd. There had been no change to the status quo since it was mentioned in the first report of the Society. In the last report of the 1970s Esmé recorded, 'Compared to progress towards a bye-law to control waterskiing on the Snowdonia Park lakes, the tortoise is a veritable Stirling Moss. Backed by the money and power of the Sports Council, the water-skiers will present a strong case. The opposition must be more than a match for them.'

And to prove that the Society was not full of 'fuddy-duddy members', Ken Jones, of Nant Peris, one of the committee members, planned, organised, and masterminded the first Snowdon race in 1976. Still a prominent and extremely popular event in the calendar today, each race begins in Llanberis with the halfway point on the Snowdon summit cairn, and the finish back at Llanberis. That first race was won by Dave Francis of Bristol in a time of one hour, twelve minutes and five seconds.

The 1979 report dealt with administrative issues too, 'Our typewriter, bought many years ago for £10 is showing signs of senile decay. If possible we would like to replace it with an electric one; such a machine would make our letters so much more attractive. Does any member have a redundant electric typewriter that they would sell to the Society for a kindly amount? We remember with gratitude how successful our appeal was for a duplicator!'

But as the 1970s end, the last paragraph of that report is full of foreboding, with the heading, 'The Nuclear Dustbin Controversy'. 'The Minister for the Environment has announced in the House of Commons that fifteen sites have been chosen to test their suitability for the burial of nuclear waste. As usual, Gwynedd is one of the fifteen. Though we are told by successive Governments that all things nuclear are absolutely safe, those who govern always show a marked preference for areas with a small population. There is seldom any nuclear development in, near, or under our large conurbations. We are all frightened of the unknown and it will require far more knowledge than is at present available before any part of the country will agree to be a nuclear waste repository.'

8

Esmé BEGAN THE first report of the new decade remarking, 'We live in an atmosphere of impending doom and will continue to do so until we can achieve legislation that will give adequate protection to our National Parks.'

At the beginning of the 1980s she felt that powerful organisations were able to exploit and develop the Park, with very little to stop them. However, the Government had promised a Parliamentary Review, but Esmé was sceptical. Was it to be another propaganda exercise, or meaningful legislation that would make the parks 'safe and inviolate' for future generations? She questioned, 'Will more and more of our National Parks disappear under the unacceptable conifers if Governments refuse to bring them under planning control? Highway departments, indifferent to the magic of Snowdonia, bulldoze their urban orientated roads through glorious scenery, with Park officials observing impotently knowing they have no power to insist on more compatible standards.'

This first report of the new decade seems to lack the energy and enthusiasm of previous reports; it's as if the fight has lost a driving force, with too many powerful organisations ready to pounce on Snowdonia and, for Esmé, the Park Authority seemingly impotent. She tells the story of one application made by the Forestry Commission to plant on the lower slopes of the Carneddau, and the effect that this has had on one family, tenants who had farmed Ffridd Goch Ganol near Dolgellau, for two hundred years.

The farm was part of the Nannau Estate and in the 1930s

the all-powerful Forestry Commission purchased part of the tenant's land. They planted conifers, and left the tenant with a paltry thirty-five acres and, instead, offered him work with the Forestry Commission. When the farmer died in 1935, his son took over the tenancy on similar terms but, when he died in 1979, the grandson's application for the tenancy was refused on the grounds of lack of experience, lack of academic farming knowledge, and because a farm of thirty-five acres was no longer a viable unit.

Esmé commented, 'A family does not give up a home that they have occupied for over two hundred years without a fight.' The family opted for a tribunal. It was the beginning of the end for those who were tenants of such small farm holdings; there was no protection unless the tenant's principal income came from agriculture. The Forestry Commission gave a concession which was, in truth, of little gain: the family would have first refusal at the sale, but the price of land was too prohibitive at that time for the tenant to contemplate buying.

Many farm dwellings came on the market at the time to be sold on as holiday homes, thus denuding local young people the opportunity to begin farming. Esmé added, 'The Forestry Commission is adopting a policy towards its tenants that is reminiscent of the heavy hand of eighteenth- and nineteenth-century landlordism.'

The tribunal was obviously sympathetic, but the law was the law, 'a tenant does not get tenancy protection unless the principle source of income is from agriculture. The life, the soul, the very existence of our small upland villages is frequently dependent on the people who live and work on the holdings.'

Another contentious issue for the Society was the proposal to build a four-lane highway along the north Wales coast – a public inquiry had sat for six months discussing it and at a cost of £2 million. The most difficult problem was how the expressway would cross the River Conwy. There were already two bridges linking the famous castle town of Conwy with Deganwy and Llandudno: the magnificent Thomas Telford suspension bridge built in 1826 and the Robert Stephenson-built railway bridge. A bridge would have been much cheaper for the A55 Expressway, but a submerged tunnel would be more acceptable to the environment, but at a cost of £15 million. The documentation landed on the Secretary of State for Wales's desk and north Wales held its breath while he considered. Industrialists and road hauliers pressed for a bridge, conservationists and local people put the case for a tunnel – it would be more expensive but would save a World Heritage site. Mr Nicholas Edwards MP announced – much to the relief of the community – that he had decided to take the expensive option; it was to be the tunnel.

Less contentious for the Society was a new venture to update a book already in circulation, *The Old Cottages of Snowdonia*, first published in 1908 by Jarvis and Foster. Two members of the Snowdonia National Park Society, Ian Stainburn and Alan Payne, decided to reappraise the material and to take new photographs in order to bring the book up to date. It was well received when it was published in 1979 ready for the Christmas market.

In 1984 Esmé became interested in its companion book, *The Old Churches of Snowdonia*, originally compiled and written by Harold Hughes and Herbert L. North in 1924. The republished version was compiled by Harvey Lloyd, and John and Elizabeth Holman, who travelled hundreds of miles visiting every church, holy well and inscribed stone. Esmé was thrilled with the book, writing, 'The Society will always be grateful to these three Society members. We know that republishing this important work will add considerably to the prestige of the Society.'

The Society's monetary outlook now seemed brighter too and that was of great satisfaction to Esmé. Membership had increased, a capital fund established with the target to raise £50,000 and, although expenditure on administration was low thanks to Esmé, future projects could not rely entirely on the goodwill and work of volunteers.

The possibility of appointing a full-time administrator had been discussed for some time. There was a need for some help to organise events, such as raising money for the capital fund. One event that Esmé suggested herself was a plant sale at Dyffryn during the Whitsun bank holiday weekend. The first sale was held in 1983, and from there on it went from strength to strength, becoming a popular event in the calendar and boosting the capital fund as well. Members brought plants, jams, cakes, pickles and chutneys to sell. As the decade came to an end, the plant sale was making £6,000 annually. A successful moneymaker, it also became an excellent social event for the Society. Lectures, walks and competitions were also organised and, when Chris Brasher and John Disley brought a wonderful supply of sports shoe seconds from their business to sell, it was another boost to the Society's capital fund.

* * *

At this time there were local physical features which were of concern to the Society. Esmé called the first, the 'beautiful menace', and the other, an 'eyesore'. Both were invaders of the landscape: one planted to show a blaze of colour in spring, and the other was an ugly, manmade, derelict building without one redeeming feature.

The rhododendron was introduced to the gardens of Aberglaslyn gorge by wealthy industrialists, but to quote Esmé, 'The acid soil and a temperate moist climate was, for them, environmental bliss. The walls around the gardens were no constraint and the wind-blown seeds spread further and further afield in the welcoming habitat.'

The rhododendron flourished through the valley bringing crowds of visitors to see the shades of pink and red in the spring. However, for the rest of the year the woody plant was a boring, monotonous, dense, dark green bush. The downside was that deciduous woods and good hill grazing land were threatened, because nothing would grow under the rhododendron bushes – the mauve menace absorbed all light and nutrition. The Park decided to begin battle by slashing the plants, an activity which occupied many people for considerable time. Slowly they uncovered the pretty gorge at Aberglaslyn. Paths were created along the River Glaslyn to take the walker to the heart of the beautiful village of Beddgelert.

The 'eyesore' was a derelict petrol station in the heart of Snowdonia, directly opposite Pen-y-Gwryd Hotel. It was finally demolished after a long campaign led by Esmé and the Society. It was built in the 1930s when the hotel owner, Arthur Lockwood, installed a small hand petrol pump on the site for the convenience of his guests. Occasionally he would sell a few gallons of petrol to passing motorists too. At the end of the war, Lockwood sold the hotel and a local entrepreneur saw development possibilities and applied to the Park committee (at the time) to enlarge the petrol station. Permission was granted. Esmé wrote, 'It was one of the worst decisions ever made by the Park committee.'

Members of the Society and many others protested vociferously. With yet another change of ownership, the petrol station was closed for long periods of time. In fact, it was closed more often than not and, by the end of the 1980s, the petrol station was put up for sale once more. It remained unsold for months and was eventually put up for auction. Once again Chris Brasher came to the rescue. He bought the filling station, lock, stock and barrel, and gave the Society the responsibility of demolishing it and landscaping the site.

Charles Quant, a respected journalist who observed and understood rural and environmental affairs, wrote at the time, 'The Snowdonia National Park Society has always been critical of the National Park Authority and some council members have publicly stated that local interests must take precedence over conservation in the Park and, of course, they have a numerical majority to support them. That attitude is reflected in the Minister's decision to grant an appeal for that horrific eyesore to be retained. Chris Brasher bought the petrol station, who gave it to the Snowdonia National Park Society to destroy it. There will be more rejoicing than the fall of the Berlin Wall.'

It would be expensive – decommissioning four redundant petrol tanks to stringent regulations and landscaping the site were beyond the Society's means. So Esmé set about looking for grants and the Welsh Development Agency gave generously and work began to reduce the petrol station to a pile of rubble. The Park Authority offered expensive mountain grass seed, a mixture that would blend in with the surrounding pasture.

A small celebration took place to commemorate the 'demise of the incongruous petrol filling station'. Chris Briggs, host at Pen-y-Gwryd for almost fifty years, planted a Welsh oak tree and placed a small plaque to record the event. The celebratory buffet was attended by those who had generously assisted the Society, especially Chris Brasher and John Disley, John Wild of the Welsh Development Agency and Alan Jones, Dr Rod Gritton and Bob Lowe of the Snowdonia National Park Authority.

* * *

Esmé was now in her seventies but, Esmé being Esmé, her energy and stamina did not flag. The campaigns, reports, meetings and conferences were unrelenting and the letter writing output constant. She would always find time to assist Will, the shepherd, at busy times. He was reliable on the farm, but his health was failing.

Dyffryn was one farming unit of 2,400 acres. In the late 1930s Esmé and her first husband had taken on the tenancy of a nearby farm, Cwm Ffynnon, owned by the Faenol Estate. In 1976 this estate was sold and all of its tenants farming the Snowdon massif area were offered first refusal to buy their farms. Esmé bought Cwm Ffynnon.

She and Peter came to the conclusion that if Will's health was failing to the extent that he wouldn't be able to continue to work, then they would have to offer the tenancy of their farmland, their sheep, cattle, outbuildings, implements and cottage to an outsider. They prepared a contract, but put the tenancy agreement on hold until Will informed them about his future.

Forward planning had always been important to Esmé and she liked being able to anticipate change. One such example: they were the first to try new systems of working or machinery; as mentioned Dyffryn was the first in the locality to buy an electric shearing machine and Esmé invited many to witness it being used the first time. There were other innovative schemes which John Morgan of the National Trust remembered, 'She was full of new ideas and when she was excited about farming ideas she'd say, "Will and I are doing this and that, always moving things forward." Everyone remembers him working with Esmé at Dyffryn and she would always start her reply with the words, "Will and I..." followed with a detailed and colourful description.'

Unfortunately Will was losing weight and it looked serious; he had tests and scans and the diagnosis was a cancerous tumour. Esmé realised that this was a turning point. Will was in his early sixties and so she could no longer rely on his fitness. The prognosis was not good either but, while he was receiving treatment, she engaged some short-term labour.

In the late autumn of 1983, with the last of the two-year-old pregnant ewes settled on the coastal farms for the winter, and the others being gathered to the *ffridd* as the winter hardened, it was obvious that Will would not return to run the farm. After a long discussion with Will and Peter, she decided, sadly, that she should offer the tenancy of Dyffryn. She placed an advertisement in the north Wales papers.

Within months Will Hughes died. He'd been known as 'Will Llandegai', that being the place of his birth. He was a loyal, courageous and a strong worker and, according to local folklore, his handsome features were such that he will be remembered too as a Burt Lancaster look-alike.

* * *

A fair number of applicants responded to the advertisement. Esmé and Peter selected a few to interview, based on their experience and knowledge of mountain farming and sheep

A young Esmé portraying two characters who have remained nameless

Esmé, aged 17, at the North Wales Golf Club founded by her father

Both in their best livery, but the terrain is difficult – no riding hat in those days

Dyffryn – the front of the farmhouse

Dyffryn – a view of both dwellings – the old cottage with the two pigsties

Esmé changed her fashion style for haymaking – cars on the A4086 stopped!

Luck, her constant companion, was allowed to peep

Occasionally, following a hard day's work in the mountains, Luck was allowed to have a lift with Googie, the pet kid

During winter snow, checking the flock was a regular necessity

Local farmers with their dogs preparing to gather the flock in the early morning

Sheep are careful of the rocky terrain of Glyder Fach

It becomes easier – crowds watch from the road

Almost 3,000 sheep being corralled safely

Experienced farmers looking at the young rams in the Dyffryn sale

Esmé is well satisfied with the day

The pens where individual sheep are counted, separated from lambs, or checked for disease

Shepherds at work

Luck keeps watch

Dinner at midday – beef stew, potatoes and rice pudding

Will Llandegai with his sheepdogs

Edna and Will with Esmé's nieces, Valerie and Jenny

Esmé walking down from the house to start the day's work

The two cottages and barns, with Snowdon in the distance

Dipping sheep
– not pleasant!

The dogs look
on as the sheep
are immersed in
a yellow liquid to
protect them from
scab

Esmé shearing with shears of the early years

... and wearing hobnailed boots to shear with electric shears

The busy day is over and others drink a last mug of tea

There is dinner to cook, just for the family…

… but there are other chores

Dressed for a day in town. L–R: Edna, Valerie, Peter, Esmé and Jenny

Sculptor Judy Greaves sitting in the seat commissioned by the Snowdonia Society to remember Esmé

A breadboard made by Peter Kirby and given as a gift to Geraint Roberts. The carvings are replicas of notches and lines on the ears of local sheep, which identify and denote the twelve farms in the local community.

husbandry, in particular the Welsh Mountain sheep. Geraint Roberts became the new tenant in September 1984; he was an experienced man who'd had a varied farming career, both practical and academic, and came from Tal-y-bont, some fifteen miles away.

'What was your first impression of Esmé?' I asked, 'Ew!' he said 'Ew, look at this photo, she was smart then, very, very smart.' He had a bundle of photographs given to him from Peter when Esmé died. He added, 'She was all right. Very fair sort of woman. She didn't keep anything from you. She was very good to me. I was her tenant for sixteen years and she didn't raise the rent or anything. No, but I didn't ask her for anything. I repaired all the fences, all the barns and sheep pens. It works both ways I suppose. She was always straight with you... no messing.'

Geraint settled in one of the cottages by the main road. He'd attended a two-year course at the Llysfasi Farm Institute and then worked on the Duke of Westminster's estate in Chester and Oswestry before buying a smallholding in Nebo near Llanrwst, where he supplemented his income as a contract fencer. Then he saw the advertisement. This was to be a challenge, the scale of the farm could be daunting but he felt he was experienced enough to overcome the difficult life in the mountains. He became a mountain farmer for twenty-seven years in total, renting from Esmé for sixteen years until she died.

Geraint and I met at the end of June. He talked much of the farming challenges at Dyffryn. 'Ponies would not be suitable here, so many stones and rocks and wet grass, and then there's bracken hiding ruts and holes. Horses, however sturdy, could easily damage their legs. What you need are good sheepdogs.'

'And I suppose you'll be shearing soon?' I asked.

'Middle of July, just before the Royal Welsh Show. I only have two or three shearers, these boys can shear three hundred sheep in a day so we'll finish in two or three days. They have a break then.' He showed photographs of shearing at Dyffryn in the 1940s and 1950s. 'At least thirty farmers coming to help, with Esmé in the middle, shearing with hand shears wearing hobnailed boots. She could handle sheep as good as anyone. And then she'd go to the house and get the food ready for everyone. Cold beef, hot potatoes and peas and rice pudding.'

I remarked, 'Every shearing day, every farmer ate rice pudding!'

He laughed so much his whole body shook, 'But Esmé made her's in a big bucket... clean of course... nice taste.' Geraint nowadays makes lunch for the three shearers himself, 'They get a good plateful.'

We talked about the price of wool. 'It has been rock bottom for some time, not worth the effort, but last year things picked up and this year, it is much better, and double last year's price.'

Esmé's nieces, Val and Jenny, also remember those sheep shearing days. They spent most holidays at Dyffryn or, as they agreed, 'She didn't look after us, we stayed there. She was always far too busy. We would come downstairs, pinch biscuits and bananas, anything. We were hungry. She was very good to us, always took us out of boarding school at half-term. She was glamorous, colourful... bright colours, mainly red. And then the sheep shearing with a rice pudding in a bucket for lunch – feeding so many people, and then the sheep sales. It was a community at work, helping each other.'

Another major event at Dyffryn was the annual sheep sale in the autumn. Geraint notes, 'It was a very good sale at the end of the traditional farming year. It was really a credit sale. Esmé was generous, she would allow farmers to buy the sheep at the September sale and pay her in six months, in March. She was getting high prices then, but she was generous as well.'

'Is the Welsh Mountain breed of sheep a bit wild and difficult?'

'Well, yes and no. Their *cynefin* – their familiar habitat, where they belong, we don't get many that go beyond their boundaries, about ten or fifteen in a year. But we can recognise them, and so can neighbouring farmers.'

Recognising and identifying sheep is a precise skill. Every farm or sheep walk has a distinctive pitch-mark placed on the backs of sheep, but the safest form is an individual notch cut into the tip of a lamb's ear, which remains there for its lifetime. These cuts are easily recognised (called *nod cyllell* – knife mark, in Welsh) and are made with a razor-sharp pocket knife, with each farm having a different design. Geraint showed me a circular breadboard, and around the edge were carvings of thirteen individual notch designs for farms in the locality, including Dyffryn. These had been carved onto the breadboard by Peter and given to Geraint when he took the tenancy.

Geraint farms in the traditional way, it's called *Hafod a Hendre* in Welsh. The farming year is divided between two locations: in winter the sheep are kept in the *Hendre*, a lowland farm. In spring and summer, they return to the *Hafod* mountain dwelling. Geraint's pregnant ewes are taken by lorry to his sister's farm near Rhyl for lush pastures and a kinder climate in the wintertime. They return to Dyffryn for the summer so that those lowland pastures can be rested. However, with rising transport costs, many farmers have nowadays invested in large sheds to house their vulnerable sheep from harsh winters.

Esmé would drive many of her sheep to the chosen wintering farms in rickety old lorries. Geraint remembers taking cattle to a sale in Anglesey in one of her lorries and seeing three or four of them put their feet through the floor!

* * *

Dry-stone walls are an attractive feature of the Snowdonia countryside. Esmé had felt that the standard of repair work was not often of the best quality. So she suggested that a competition would promote interest in this ancient craft. Building walls to enclose tracts of land, such as the *ffridd* on Glyder Fach at Dyffryn, is done to define the boundaries and to protect sheep and cattle on open mountains. Walls are built of stones of varying size and shape which have been gathered from the land. No mud or cement holds them together, so it's a natural and sustainable way of building walls on difficult terrain. They are costly to maintain, but their visual impact adds to the landscape, whereas a wired fence seems an imposition on the scenery.

A good number of spectators turned up to watch the first competition held on 1 October 1983 at Dyffryn. A great deal of luck is involved in every competition as each competitor draws for his six-foot-length 'stint' – one stint may have good walling stones, yet the next might be a pile of stones which could include a few awkward ones. Competitors young and old, professional and amateur, got on with the job in hand, and it was a skill that was appreciated by the local community. All the winners of the first competition were in their twenties. The enthusiasm was such that the Society decided to make it an annual event and, as a consequence, a dry-stone wall association was established in Gwynedd by enthusiastic practitioners.

* * *

Perhaps the most treasured resources in Snowdonia are the minerals hidden deep beneath the surface. There's evidence that mining for copper and gold started with the Neolithic population of the Bronze and Iron Ages. Serious excavation began with the Romans in AD 75, who then fashioned gold torques and armbands in beautiful workmanship. The Welsh princes also became rulers with considerable wealth and power due to the rich supplies of ores, such as the gold found in an area stretching from Barmouth to Dolgellau. Today Welsh gold is considered the most exclusive in the world, three times the price of ordinary gold. Two mines, in particular, were responsible for producing the precious metal, Clogau and Gwynfynydd.

Gwynfynydd was a gold mine located in the village of Ganllwyd, between Dolgellau and Trawsfynydd. It began mining in 1862 and was active until 1998. Clogau, located in the small village of Bont-ddu overlooking the Mawddach estuary, began mining for copper and gold the same year. It became the largest and most productive mine in the area, but closed in 1911. Although reopened several times, it's been for smaller-scale operations. During one such scheme a large nugget of gold was brought up to the surface and was presented to the royal family. From that nugget all rings for royal weddings have since been made.

A developer tried to create a tourist attraction in Clogau in the 1980s. He heralded that it would become the largest visitor attraction in Wales. However, even before the developer had received official agreement from planners, he decided to begin work on a car park, devastating a woodland area in the centre of Bont-ddu in the process. He apologised and tried to convince the villagers that the damage was superficial, reminding them that he estimated that 250,000 tourists would visit the attraction annually. They would be carried in a cabin-lift (he called it a gondola) to the site. The scheme, to everyone's surprise, was scheduled to go before the Park planning committee on 14 October 1987 and the feeling among the committee members was apparently positive and in favour. Esmé sent two letters objecting to the scheme, in line with the Council for National Parks, the Countryside Commission, and local people who were vehemently against the idea. As time went on, the Secretary of State for Wales said that the matter was of national interest and that a public inquiry was justified. Two years later, on 10 August 1989, came the decision '... That planning permission be refused... and the Secretary of State for Wales accepts his recommendation.'

This reversal was based on environmental factors, although it was acknowledged that visitors might find the gondola ride and a visit to the mine interesting. A few jobs, though nothing like the number claimed by the applicant, would bring some economic benefit to Barmouth and Dolgellau, but the damage it would do to one of the most beautiful areas of the Park, 'one of the jewels in Snowdonia's crown', outweighed the commercial benefits.

No-one was more pleased by this turnaround than Esmé. She had persuaded members of the Society and around eight hundred influential friends to write letters to the inspector of the public inquiry. Her own letter writing increased too at this time, with many in authority irritated and tired of her persistent questions and criticisms; a few even refused to answer her letters. Members of the Society too queried the volume of work she was taking on. Now, with the capital fund nearing its target of £50,000, she bowed to pressure from the committee and an administrator was appointed.

Jenny James was soon in post; she was young and capable, with wide knowledge and experience but, however much she respected Esmé as the chair, she soon realised that Esmé would be reluctant to delegate work to her. One solution was to move the office away from Dyffryn. The workload was increasing and the Countryside Commission had, for some time, been pushing the Society to become a professionally structured organisation. Many committee members also agreed that the office should be moved away from Dyffryn and that the Society, in time, should have a remunerated director.

However, within two and a half years Jenny James resigned. Her contribution was applauded; she had been mainly responsible for steering 'The Young Snowdonians', increasing their number to one hundred and fifty members. This group was organised mainly through its own newsletter, enthusiastically tackling many aspects of conservation work among the young, such as planting trees and digging ditches.

The search for suitable office space continued, with Esmé stubbornly persisting that Dyffryn was the suitable location for it. David Firth explained, 'Esmé was against it, not because it was taking power away from Dyffryn, but because it was going to cost money.' However, she was prepared to look round for a suitable building and, in time, the Countryside Commission gave the Society a grant for this purpose.

Esmé often discussed the future of the Society with Alan Jones, the Snowdonia National Park officer, but occasionally they took opposing views, as in the example of the Clogau attraction. 'She was a preservationist – wanting to keep Snowdonia as it was. A few hated her guts because they thought she was against every proposal, and she did oppose most industrial or commercial developments which would bring work to the area, and a few that would need skilled labour with good wages.' Those discussions with Alan Jones were, '… real ding-dongs. But on a personal level we were very friendly. They were arguments, not quarrels.'

Although Esmé was not a member of the National Park committee, she attended most of their meetings sitting in the same chair at every meeting – Esmé's chair – contributing when she had a statement to make, which was always well thought out and researched.

The issue of a suitable building for the Society's office intensified. Mike Cousins, a local man who lived in Capel Curig, mentioned that Tŷ Hyll (the Ugly House), not too far from Betws-y-coed and Capel Curig on the A5, was on the market. The dwelling, which had been empty for many years, was almost derelict. Tŷ Hyll was well known for its small size and was built of a rugged stone structure, with a few of its small boulders weighing up to four tons each. Esmé consulted David Firth, her vice-chairman, and received a positive endorsement to negotiate a price reduction for the cottage with its owners. She foresaw the possibility of making money in this plan, with an office for the administrators and a small museum where they could charge for entry.

The restoration would be costly, estimated at £50,000. However, Peter Kirby proposed that he could save the Society £30,000 if he oversaw members and others doing the work in a voluntary capacity. So, the Society took the risk, and the deal to purchase Tŷ Hyll was completed on 8 July 1988. It was announced at a splendid dinner to mark the Society's twenty-first birthday. Esmé told the gathering, 'It gives us an opportunity not only to have a wonderful headquarters but to save an important part of Welsh heritage.'

Tŷ Hyll's past is shrouded in mystery but it is thought that it dated back to the fifteenth century. The most recent owners, Edward Riley and his wife Lillian, had bought the cottage in 1928; it was a convenient home as he worked at the Towers Outdoor Education Centre next door. The couple lived there until he died in 1961, when the property was then left to relatives. The cottage changed hands frequently in the next few years and became a tea room and an antiques shop, only to then close and remain empty.

Once bought, Esmé and Peter resolved that the renovation of Tŷ Hyll would be completed by Easter 1989. Working against the clock, Peter prepared a detailed plan, and renovation work began in October 1988. Esmé wrote, 'His problems were many, the four walls were of different length and of different height. The slates and rotting roof timbers were removed and replaced with 7,000 tiny thick slates, new beams were re-hung, and manoeuvring them into position in the huge boulders was a real feat.' Peter designed, made and installed a fine oak staircase. In addition to supervising the old-style plastering downstairs, he also found stone slabs for the ground floor. The Welsh Folk Museum at St Fagans, near Cardiff, was persuaded to lend suitable cottage kitchen furniture for part of the ground floor, which was also turned into a small museum and shop.

Esmé was not really interested in providing space and facilities for staff, and as the committee began the task of appointing a director for the Society, she vehemently resented that the new post would be salaried. When the committee came to discuss working hours and agreements, she could not agree with them. As David Firth told me,

'Members of the committee were shocked at her intransigent attitude; there were discussions and disagreements which became so unpleasant that many left the committee. Worse, no-one would come and work for the Society, and all of this was due to Esmé's attitude and manner. She expected staff to work for very little, more likely for nothing.'

Peter oversaw the renovation work completed on time, but as Esmé wrote, 'He made one mistake. He had estimated that it could be done for £19,800. In fact he did it for less than £15,000.' John Irving, the Society's treasurer, told the story of how the rebuilding work began in October 1988 and ended, as promised by Peter working with a cohort of volunteers, by Easter 1989. The two floors were linked by a fine oak staircase, with workmanship of the first order. With the cottage now ready to be furnished, the move from Dyffryn to Tŷ Hyll was completed. In the 1989 annual report, Esmé was prompted to say, 'Congratulations Peter. You more than deserve all the compliments you have received, especially from architects, builders and joiners who can appreciate the problems you faced and admired your skilful work.'

The cottage had been saved and transformed. The ground floor was initially used as a museum, but it evolved into an exhibition area for the Society's work. The upper floor accommodated the staff. The Society's office moved from Dyffryn to Tŷ Hyll, and it was 'the end of an era'. New office equipment, a computer, and a photocopier were installed which made the Society more efficient and administrative work less time-consuming. But, words of warning came from Esmé, 'Of one thing you can be certain. Routine office work may be mechanised but NEVER, NEVER will members receive computerised replies to their letters. We value too highly the personal interest that you take in the

Society. We may never have met but many of you are like old friends and long may it continue.'

Esmé called Tŷ Hyll 'Our Window on the World'. The garden and woodland, about five acres in total, had become a wilderness. So three Society members – known as 'The Gnomes of Tŷ Hyll', Neville and Pam Jones and Daphne Taylor – met on the first Monday of every month to transform the garden, first into a cottage garden and then it became the Snowdonia Wildlife Gardening Partnership. Paths were reinstated or constructed throughout the woodland at the back of house by Donald Campbell, with the help of a group of boys from Bromsgrove School, and a woodland management scheme planned. The British Trust for Ornithology installed and monitored sixteen bird boxes, attracting blue and great tits and pied flycatchers among many others. Tŷ Hyll may have seemed to be a window on the world but it was also an outpost of the activities of Society volunteers too.

9

THE SOCIETY BEGAN looking for a director during its coming of age year, 1988. 'This appointment' Esmé wrote, 'will be of supreme importance. The future of the Society will depend on our choice and the right person must be found. It must be someone capable of considerable dedication who will regard the work as a way of life.'

But idealism was not matched by realism, especially when the Society had been led by a chairwoman who had a mountain of strengths and had set ground rules, yet so many times had failed to delegate herself. A paid official working in a voluntary organisation could find such a relationship uncomfortable. The Snowdonia National Park Society had over 3,000 members by now.

Richard Hills was appointed the first director; he was followed by Paul Wakely and Tony Shaw, each one with admirable qualities and qualifications. However, the three directors vacated the hot seat quite quickly, creating a perceived crisis, and the press soon diagnosed the problem...

Esmé also realised that there was a problem, but only when she read a critical letter in the local press about the Society and, in particular, its leadership. It had been written by Tony Shaw, the third and latest director to leave, and she recognised that the thrust of his criticism was directed at her. She was angry and hurt. Many members were steadfastly loyal to Esmé but there was a growing number who felt the time had come for a change at the top of the Society. Ruth Cox, who had been secretary to the director, carried on with the everyday administrative affairs throughout all the comings and goings.

* * *

At this tumultuous time Esmé tried to focus her attention on the main campaigns and one which exercised her was the Cwm Dyli pipeline. This was a double pipe placed originally in 1906 to carry water from Llyn Llydaw, hidden in the horseshoe of Mount Snowdon, down to the small power station in the Nant Gwynant Valley (affectionately known due to its design, as the Chapel in the Valley). The Central Electricity Generating Board (CEGB) proposed replacing the pipes with one large pipe, four feet in diameter, which would be held in a two-foot-high cradle. The cost of the project was estimated at £3.6 million, and was to include a more efficient turbine to increase productivity and to provide an income of £500,000 for the electricity company.

Esmé thought that this was a good opportunity to bury the new pipe underground for the sake of the environment. However, she soon realised that the CEGB had no such intention. The electricity board had looked at the cost and decided that that option would be too expensive, at an extra £2.5 million. The pipe was a mile long, and for anyone travelling up the valley on the A498 from Beddgelert to Pen-y-Gwryd, the view of Snowdon would be blemished forever. As Dr Rod Hackney, president of the Snowdonia National Park Society noted, 'The replacement pipe will still be there for all to see, as a monument to greed, avarice, short term-ism and sheer obstinacy.'

Esmé campaigned by letter, telephone, distribution of leaflets and meetings with Peter Walker, the Secretary of State for Wales; Wyn Roberts, the Minister of State; Dr David Owen, the SDP Leader; and Cecil Parkinson, the Secretary of State for the Energy. However the CEGB remained intransigent, although everyone knew that they had managed to bury the hydro-electric scheme inside Elidir Fawr mountain, the largest pumped storage scheme in Europe. So why not bury the replacement pipe? The CEGB stood firm; there was no about turn.

As a last resort, the Society's president and Esmé decided to meet the hierarchy of CEGB on their own territory. At a meeting Lord Marshall of Goring, its chairman, sat at the top of an oval table surrounded by twenty of the company's senior executives. Esmé stood up and gazed at the chairman, directing her comments at him. 'That scar' she said, 'will lie across the Snowdon scene for the next hundred years; don't let it be on your conscience that you did nothing about it.'

Lord Marshall was well briefed and responded that the estimated extra cost for the new designs, costly contracts to be renegotiated, and delay, would amount to £5 million. Secondly, the Snowdonia National Park Society was the 'only main objector'; the CEGB had canvassed views from five hundred people who had written that they did not want the Nant Gwynant Valley power station to close (a possibility if the pipe wasn't replaced), with the loss of employment opportunities.

Lord Marshall was a man of principle and to him that was more satisfying than bending to someone else's opinion. Six months later the scheme went ahead although the letter writing continued. When the pipe, resting on its concrete cradle, was in its place and fully operational, the community slowly realised that the power station was fully automated, so no local employment was created.

The scar on the lower slopes of Snowdonia remains as prominent today as it was when the pipe was placed. There was no attempt to hide the monstrous construction on such a unique mountain landscape. Esmé was right all along, but the campaign failed.

The Conservative government later decided to privatise the CEGB and divide the large organisation into three: National Power, Powergen and Nuclear Power but, after many deliberations, Nuclear Power was kept in public hands. Chernobyl, the catastrophic disaster at a nuclear station in the Ukraine in 1986, released large quantities of radioactive contamination into the atmosphere which spread over western USSR and Europe. Snowdonia sheep farmers suffered most, and even today certain areas remain subject to regular inspection for caesium and strontium in the soil.

* * *

As the 1980s came to a close, the new Secretary of State for the Environment, Christopher Patten, inaugurated a Countryside Commission review of the ten national parks. The Commission appointed a committee to review progress, or the lack of it, of the implementation of the 1949 National Parks and Access to the Countryside Act, and to present a report to Parliament in the autumn of 1991.

Firstly, the Society set to work on their submission to the Park Authority. They argued that agriculture and commercial afforestation should come under effective planning control; roads should fit the landscape; with regard to tourism, it should never be forgotten that it was the *beauty* of the Park which attracted visitors; footpaths and bridleways should be under the control of the Park Authority and not under the jurisdiction of the Gwynedd County Council, and so on.

'The Parks as we know them have no future unless

95

Government, whatever colour, passes firm and effective legislation to protect them. The unspoilt future of this precious heritage is in their hands,' Esmé wrote in the submission.

The Sandford Report, a similar review of National Park progress, published in 1974, noted 'the increasing conflict between recreation and conservation, and between national parks and other government agencies.' It concluded that good planning and management could resolve most complaints, but when enjoyment and conservation could not be reconciled, conservation should take priority.

It became known as the Sandford Principle. The Government had long endorsed the principle, but did not attempt to legislate until the 1991 review had been concluded. Conservation had moved up the political agenda and the review committee, chaired by Professor Ron Edwards, endorsed the Sandford Principle, together with other recommendations which had been shelved for far too long. In 1991 it was recommended that the Snowdonia National Park be an organisation independent of Gwynedd County Council's interference.

Esmé was pleased, but she realised that the membership of the Park's new Board would include many councillors who believed their first duty would be to those who voted them into office.

The Countryside Commission's report entitled 'Fit for the Future' included the statutory purposes of the Park:

a) To preserve and enhance the natural beauty of the Parks.
b) To promote their quiet enjoyment by the public.
c) When there is conflict, conservation must have priority.

Although the Government had let it be known that legislation for a new National Park Bill was due in the autumn of 1992, it was not mentioned in the Queen's Speech.

The Society reiterated, 'that new legislation could make a tremendous difference to see Snowdonia treated with that special care it so richly deserves.'

The greatest threat facing the Snowdonia National Park Authority was the Government proposal to reform local government once more. The Secretary of State for Wales intended putting a Bill before Parliament to provide Wales with unitary authorities in the spring of 1995.

But long before that change, the Society went through its own period of turbulence, at a time when it was approaching another chapter in its history – the twenty-fifth anniversary – the silver jubilee.

* * *

On the last day of August 1990, there was a surprise for Esmé as she turned eighty. Peter had organised to take her to lunch. They crossed the Menai Straits to Anglesey and travelled across the island to Valley, and there she was told to enter a Sea King helicopter. Off they flew to Castell y Gwynt on Glyder Fach, which Esmé had climbed so often to gather her flock when she was a full-time shepherd. Many of her friends were there waiting for her to cut a birthday cake and to celebrate a memorable occasion, 'on high', for a remarkable woman.

10

Since she established the Snowdonia National Park Society in 1967, Esmé, as chairman, had written almost every annual report in her own distinctive style. They were not always an objective record of all activities; they were factual, yet entertaining, much like her letters. In what turned out to be her last report in 1991, written before the annual general meeting, there is almost a defiant tone and the message is stark:

'This is the chairman's report to the members of the Snowdonia National Park Society and does not necessarily represent the views of the officers or executive committee. It is entitled "Au Revoir". For twenty years or so the committee have entrusted me to write the annual report for the Society. They have given me a good run and I am grateful for their tolerance. In any case, they only pre-empt the inevitable by 'x' number of years. I'm well into the "drop dead at any minute age group", and there is a useful strain of angina in the family. The beginning of this dissertation says au revoir, not goodbye. I shall continue as chairman as long as members wish me to do so, but it is high time you members found someone to take my place with sufficient time, enthusiasm and competence to do all the work involved as chairman of this successful and active Society.'

Esmé's report went on to cover eighteen topics, policies and schemes in her usual direct and colourful language. Heading the list was the Padog Bends (and more on that later); then, wind farms: 'these look like being the problem children of the future;' then, the Strategy for Gwynedd – a mission statement from Gwynedd County Council (fifty-eight per cent of Gwynedd is in the Park) provoked this statement: 'Reading it gave us a shock. The great mission statement did not once mention the Park – not once! ... It's That Pipe Again – too late, the Park Authority is worried about the Cwm Dyli Pipe. They built a special viewpoint for us to enjoy the magnificent panorama of the mountains of Eryri and then allowed the awful pipe to dominate centre stage.'

The update of Tŷ Hyll was next: 'When we bought the little cottage, the garden was an overgrown wilderness. Thanks to the Gnomes and especially to Neville and Pam Jones, the King and Queen of Gnomes, the garden has made good progress but there is still much to be done.' The National Park review panel brought about the following remark: 'On the whole it is a good review but remembering other reports and reviews, how much of this will be implemented? The review was unanimously in favour of Boards in the Parks so that they would be independent of their various county councils. Though independent boards would be a great step forward, councillors believed their first duty was to those who voted them onto their respective local authorities.' Near the end of her report she notes in bold capitals for emphasis:

STOP PRESS:
SNOWDONIA WILL BECOME AN INDEPENDENT BOARD

That was her wish and her command as she was about to face the first challenge to her chairmanship, but her last thoughts as she wrote her au revoir were for, 'Two grand old men of the mountains who died in 1991. In July our own Evan Roberts, aged eighty-eight, of Capel Curig, the village he had spent all his life. A remarkable man. Living the hard life of a quarryman until he was forty-four when he developed silicosis. Undaunted, he joined the newly formed Nature Conservancy Council and became their first warden at Cwm Idwal. In this post he was able to pursue the great love of his life, the study of the mountain flora of Snowdonia. Though he went blind in later years, his cheery smile and delight in living never left him and the tall figure with his white stick was a familiar sight in the village. We miss him.

"AW', as Alfred Wainwright liked to be called, was almost as famous as his beloved Lakeland hills. It is not so well known that he made several forays into north Wales and visited us at our home on the side of the Glyders when he was working on his Snowdonia books, *A North Wales Sketchbook* and *Welsh Mountain Drawings*. He was a generous member of the Society for many years and one year sent us some of his original north Wales sketches to sell at our plant sale. He became seriously ill and went into hospital early this year. AW knew that his time had run out. He removed all medical contraptions, demanded a supper of fried fish and mushy peas and went to see if the promised paradise was more beautiful than his beloved Lakeland. A lovely quirky man. He must have inspired love of the hills in more people than any other man.'

And Esmé's final thought on the future in that 1991 report:

'The 1991 AGM may be a momentous occasion for the Society. Whether decisions made on that day are the best for the Society and Snowdonia may depend on you, the members – so please do attend. I know there are several "Notices of Motion", some of which may be contentious. If voting takes place, think carefully before you vote. Ask yourself this simple all-important question "What is best for the Snowdonia National Park Society and its work for Snowdonia?" – AND VOTE FOR IT.'

* * *

There were occasions when Esmé went against decisions made by the Society's executive committee. This kind of action caused frustration and animosity which led to an eventual split in the membership.

As already mentioned, directors appointed in good faith left soon after unable to, '... handle Esmé's interference and criticism, it reduced the Society's effectiveness as an organisation,' according to Rob Collister in book published for the Society's twenty-fifth anniversary, *Snowdonia – Park Under Pressure.*

Matters came to a head in the months before that annual general meeting in 1991. Vice-chairman David Firth recognised that the leadership of the society was receiving considerable criticism, especially in its financial management. Over the years the Society had accumulated a significant amount of money which wasn't being used. Members believed that purchasing and moving to Tŷ Hyll would be the opportunity for several salaried professional staff to administrate the Society.

Change was necessary and it was at this point that David Firth was persuaded to stand for election as chairman. He had enormous respect for Esmé from that very first day he met her when she persuaded him to join the Society. 'For me it was a life-changing moment. I came to Snowdonia to teach outdoor pursuits at Plas y Brenin. I went to a public meeting held by the Park Authority gathering views on a new plan for the Park. At that time I was interested in countryside activities, walking, mountain climbing and canoeing, not a great interest in flora and fauna. But when I came to this valley, Aberglaslyn, I immediately felt a community feeling. I got to know more people here in four months than I did in four years in Haywards Heath, Sussex.'

Serious divisions continued throughout the summer of 1991 and as the date of the annual general meeting, Saturday, 19 October, approached, Esmé realised that many members were proposing to nominate another candidate for the chair. However she had no intention of stepping aside. She knew she had many loyal supporters; she was ready for an election, ready for a fight. It would be awkward for both candidates.

David Firth vividly remembers the occasion. 'Esmé was my mentor, I didn't expect all of this, but they said, look, you're the only person who can stand against Esmé, which really shocked me... it was all very painful and upsetting.'

David and I sat in his lovely house in Beddgelert as he recalled the day of that meeting in October 1991. The meeting was held at Neuadd Idris, Dolgellau. A large crowd, around two hundred and fifty people, had gathered by two o'clock in the afternoon and a buzz of excitement or apprehension went around the hall as they waited for proceedings to begin. Many believed Esmé would not be chair for much longer and, at 2.22 p.m. precisely, the Society's president, Dr Rod Hackney, stood on his feet to call the meeting to order.

In twenty-five years there had never been the need for an election for a new chairman and there was widespread interest in the result. The president asked the members whether the press should be allowed to be present throughout the meeting; he received a unanimous agreement that they should.

Firstly, Dr Hackney quoted the relevant paragraphs of the

constitution, a reminder of the aims and principles of the Society's values and achievements:

> To work to conserve the scenery, the natural and historic features, and the wildlife within the Parkland, to keep them unimpaired for the enjoyment of present and future generations.
>
> To promote reconciliation of the various land uses and interests within the Park and to work for mutual understanding between all people who visit, live and work in the Park.
>
> To persuade the authorities concerned to make public their plans for the Park, to see that those plans are compatible and to watch that they are consistently applied; but the Society may disagree with any plan, or any part of it, or its application in any particular case.
>
> To cooperate with individuals, other organisations and statutory bodies, in order to achieve these objects.

The treasurer's report followed, and Esmé's 'Chairman's Report' which had already been widely circulated. Many members were keen to query almost every sentence. However, it was the resignation of Tony Shaw, the Society's director, and the critical letter he'd written to the press, together with subsequent comments, which caused a prolonged question and answer session.

The tension and temperature in the hall increased as they reached the last item – the election of officers. Dr Rod Hackney was confirmed almost unanimously to be president, but procedures for the election of chairman became entangled between those who wished to see change and those who preferred the status quo. Two names had been nominated and following a secret ballot the result was announced: E. Kirby – 110; D. Firth – 138, with two spoilt papers.

Esmé's response was, 'If you can use me again, it's fine by me. I will now have time to put my own chaotic affairs in order.' Dr Hackney immediately proposed that the founder of the Snowdonia National Park Society should take the title of consultant and Esmé answered, 'I've done my stint and we do want fresh ideas into the Nineties. I'm quite happy to act as consultant.'

Chris Brasher paid his own tribute, 'There would be no Society without Esmé. We need you Esmé and Snowdonia needs you for the future.' Esmé made this pledge, 'I shall try and keep my mouth shut, but if I think they are not doing something right, I won't be able to resist getting them to change their minds.'

That was not the end of the afternoon's deliberations. There was considerable confusion regarding the procedures for electing committee members because of a lack of clarity in the constitution. A proposal suggested that all committee members should resign and put themselves up for re-election. Despite many questions and objections about procedures, the election of members went ahead. Peter Kirby was re-elected as a committee member, and a number of Esmé's supporters. Lord Dafydd Elis-Thomas accepted the role of vice-chairman; with the following adopted unopposed: honorary secretary, Peter Couch, and treasurer, Jim Irving. The meeting ended at 7.15 p.m.

Members of the press surrounded David Firth, the new chairman. Cameras flashed and questions were fired, 'How do you feel now that you have beaten Esmé Kirby, the founder of the Society?' He stumbled to the answer, it was not easy to find the right words, 'Pleased at the size of the vote but Esmé has been my mentor in so many ways since I joined the Society and I'm grateful. The Society will change and must now move on.'

The result of the election for chairman was brutal for Esmé and there was little anyone could do in the immediate aftermath. Her husband and her close friends listened and commiserated, but the disappointment was keenly felt in the privacy of Dyffryn. Esmé knew she would find it difficult to accept such a momentous change in her status after nearly twenty-five years of hard work and Peter could do no more than comfort her. Her loyal supporters sustained her too. This was her long reply to one member's letter five days later:

> It was kind of you to write such a heart-warming letter. I have been proud and happy to serve Snowdonia ever since the Society was founded in 1967. I didn't give a damn about losing the chair, you will know I only wanted to continue until the possible new committee was happily established... it was essential to get rid of the remnants of the old committee. It was down to seven members, two reliable supporters of the Society but hopelessly outnumbered by five whose only interest in life was to get rid of the b****y chairman, hence the reason for my drastic resolution to get rid of the present committee.
>
> With help and guidance from many people I submitted a list of prospective members, I proposed twelve names, and, as you know it worked like a charm, I think members trusted me. Nine of my nominees were returned and three were unable to be present at the meeting. Always fatal, absent nominees seldom get elected... I feel very happy. These last weeks have been rather traumatic but the outcome is a triumph.
>
> Floreat Snowdonia
> As ever
> Esmé

* * *

The new chairman immediately advertised for a new director. Martyn Evans, the successful candidate, was able to join the Society in April 1992 as an administrator. In a short time he became the public voice of the Society in

Welsh and English, giving a fresh perspective on the work and policies of the Society. That was enough of a clue for Esmé to realise that one major change had been accepted, that the Society was now a bilingual society. The chairman insisted that official papers, notably the public document, the annual report 1992, would be issued in Welsh and English. The local community welcomed this bilingual policy, shown best perhaps with record amount of entries being submitted for the dry-stone walling competition the following year. The Society also announced a new competition, its Eryri Farming and Landscape Award, hoping that this would attract many who were interested in encouraging wildlife habitats, field boundaries, footpaths and water features.

However, as time passed Esmé persisted in interfering in the affairs of the Tŷ Hyll office, prompting Martyn Evans to warn David Firth that she was undermining the chairman's authority. Her questioning continued to cause a split in the Society and it was obvious that she had one aim in mind – to win the next election.

* * *

A major celebration was imminent, the Society had reached its twenty-fifth anniversary in 1992, and there was a tacit agreement that the time had come to put differences aside to honour the Society's founder. The plans were to make a weekend of it, and the invitation to members advocated: 'Our twenty-fifth anniversary is no time to be alone, so come and rejoice in the festivities along with other members.' A dinner was served at the Grand Hall in Penrhyn Castle for members and guests. Among them were Alan Jones of the National Park who had worked closely with the Society; Professor Ian Mercer, chief executive of the Countryside Council for

Wales and Peter Broomhead, the regional director of the National Trust's north-west region. It was a grand occasion with almost a hundred people enjoying the festivities and speeches.

Mount Snowdon was the natural rendezvous to close the celebrations. On the Sunday, half the gathering walked together to the summit, with the others taking the train. It was not a bright day; the walkers experienced thick mist and cloud but, as they reached the summit, there was brilliant sunshine and Esmé was ready to cut the first slice of the large cake baked and decorated by Joan Firth. The weekend had been a success. They all stood above the mist and cloud where they could enjoy the beauty and strength of Snowdon.

* * *

There are many routes up to the summit of Snowdon which allow walkers to take regular backward glances to appreciate the different perspectives of the mountain. Two of the most popular routes begin from the east, the Pen-y-Pass/Gwryd (PyG), and the well-worn industrial route to Llyn Llydaw following the miners' path to the Brittania Copper Mine. From the west the route begins at the village of Rhyd-ddu. These paths are all well used and the Park Authority maintains them in good repair, but unfortunately many visitors take risks, wearing unsuitable clothes and flimsy footwear. With often capricious weather, clouds gathering almost without warning, it adds to the dangers of dropping temperatures and high winds on top of the annual two hundred inches of rain which falls in the area.

The most expensive route up the mountain is by the Snowdon Mountain Railway. The track was placed in 1896 and it was a Victorian era engineering feat. The diesel engine climbs 4.7 miles from Llanberis to the summit, at a gradient of one in five at times, and stops at four halts: Hebron, where there is a small chapel; Halfway, which explains itself; Clogwyn, where the driver decides whether to proceed by checking the wind speed at the summit, and finally the terminus at the top, Rocky Valley Halt. Passengers do not alight at these halts but these do allow trains to pass each.

In 1898 the station was erected at the summit, followed by a small hotel which was demolished in the 1930s to be replaced by a restaurant designed by the Welsh architect, Clough Williams-Ellis. The number of visitors increased as the decades passed, with the restaurant being subjected to a battering from the elements. The Prince of Wales once described the site as the 'highest slum in Wales'. So an urgent campaign began to improve the facilities on the summit and in June 2009 a splendid building at a cost of £8.4 million was opened on the site. It was given the name, *Hafod Eryri* (The High Home of Snowdon).

I asked David Firth about Esmé's opinion of the old building and the possibility of a new building. Did she have a vision?

'If she had a vision, she didn't want change. She certainly didn't like the old Clough Williams-Ellis building; she wanted the mountain to stay as it was. I would say that's the attitude of a preservationist, not a conservationist... we have to have change, but more important is how we manage that change and I don't really think Esmé ever understood the point.'

'What would she have thought of the new building?'

'Oh, she wouldn't have liked it, too modern, too new. I have no doubts about that. But then, she didn't like the old building, although she did accept the need for a new one. She was frail and old at the twenty-fifth celebrations, bright as a button, but she took the celebratory cake cooked by Joan on the train to reach the summit. She had no difficulty using the building and, yet, she didn't agree with it.'

* * *

The two-day celebration for the twenty-fifth anniversary in 1992 had given Esmé a boost. One enlightened major decision made by the Society was to give a substantial financial gift which would enhance the landscape, safeguard against development and preserve hill farming practices in Snowdonia. Therefore the Society gave the National Trust £1,000 for each year of its lifetime, a contribution of £25,000 to help buy the 1,000-acre farm, Hafod y Porth, in Nant Gwynant, near Beddgelert. The Chris Brasher Trust gave a further £75,000, enabling the purchase which included a copper mine, a small caravan park and an ancient hill-top fort, Dinas Emrys, with its associations to King Arthur and Llywelyn the Great.

11

THE NEWLY-ELECTED EXECUTIVE began to establish several sub-committees on specific subjects to make good use of the expertise among its thousands of members. In turn, these sub-committees made recommendations to the main committee.

Many of the topics and policies discussed throughout the summer and early autumn of 1992 were based on Snowdonia National Park Authority's document, 'Eryri's Future – Issues for Discussion'. The Park's aim was to create a new strategic five-year plan to provide a clear legal framework for the management of the Park. Such a plan would have projections for growth, economic development, housing, mineral extraction, waste regulation and environmental priorities within the whole Park.

The Society responded to a few of these policies, in particular the visitor impact on existing popular places and the identification of popular visitor areas in the future. The Society felt that there was a need for a management plan which would improve footpaths, erosion and infrastructure in those areas. The Park, the Society presumed, would be against any single, large-scale development which could threaten its environmental character.

David Firth was a very different kind of chairman of the Society to Esmé. She'd been a vocal campaigner, always leading from the front, enjoying battles in the public domain. David was just as knowledgeable, but he took another route to achieve his goals. He knew his politics, local and national, but he avoided publicity until he was sure that he had uncovered all problems, discussed them with other interested organisations, and only then, when he was convinced he had support, would he present his case to the public. This does not mean that Esmé didn't do any research – she read widely: reports, articles and plans. She would consult her allies and influential friends mainly and she would feed the media with her intentions to build up for the battle.

* * *

She has been compared to Octavia Hill who, together with Sir Robert Hunter and Canon H. D. Rawnsley, bought and established the first piece of land in Barmouth for the National Trust. Octavia Hill is revered for her vision. These three individuals wanted an organisation of members to protect distinctive ancient buildings, from small cottages to terraced houses and grand mansions and estates. Octavia Hill's motivation was to create 'an outdoor sitting-room for the poor', for people who never saw an open piece of green land in dark industrial Britain; she wanted everyone to have access to beautiful places and fresh air and new experiences.

Esmé, for all her success, was respected but not necessarily revered.

* * *

Even though she no longer had a leading role in the Society she'd established, this didn't stop her from continuing to campaign. Imminent major projects for improving roads exercised her, in particular the plans for the A5 route, the main artery from England to Wales.

The new dual-carriageway, the A55, along the north Wales coast had certainly lessened the volume of traffic using the old A5 route through the mountains within the Park. But the twisty bends on the road running through the gorges near Betws-y-coed remained dangerous to drivers, so a consultation process to straighten the road was set up by the Welsh Office highways directorate.

Esmé's reaction to that section of the A5 plan, a £5.6 million scheme known as the Padog Bends was simple, short and to the point, 'Plans for another monstrous road scheme is about to be inflicted on Snowdonia.'

Esmé set to work immediately, writing and calling members of the Houses of Parliament and Lords, organisations such as the National Trust, Countryside Commission, CPRW, National Farmers Union, and so on. Lord Hunt, the ex-Secretary of State for Wales, tabled a question in the House of Lords condemning the scheme, and he found many others to support him. Esmé's letter to the *Independent* newspaper dated 14 February 1993, was headed, 'Road Scheme is Round the Bend'. She writes:

> In his statement concerning the A5 Snowdonia Padog Bends, the Minister of State, Welsh Office, Sir Wyn Roberts has been given out-of-date statistics. He says, 'The improvement is necessary because there were twenty-five accidents on that stretch between 1987 and 1991'.
>
> These figures were before the Conwy Tunnel was opened by the Queen in October 1991. Since then traffic on the A5 has dropped so dramatically that only two accidents, one classed as serious, one slight, have occurred at the Padog Bends.
>
> On these figures, can the expenditure of £5.6 million (1990) be justified on a 1.5 mile section of road?
>
> Esmé Kirby,
> Snowdonia National Park Society

The National Park Authority supported the stance by Esmé and the Society but Gwynedd County Council strongly refused to endorse the Authority's viewpoint. The Snowdonia National Park Society further listed their concerns about the plan for the A5:

> The straightening of the Padog Bends will encourage cars and heavy goods vehicles to travel faster through that particular area making it, in our view, even more dangerous than it presently is – we would like to see the 'easing' of bends in keeping with the character of the road.
>
> The bypass route for Bethesda preferred by the Welsh Office is not the most environmentally friendly or the most cost effective.
>
> The Society would like to see the Welsh Office prepare an overall strategy for the A5 to reflect safety aspects, environmental considerations and its true strategic value.

In March 1997, following many discussions, inquiries, surveys, reports and persistent lobbying, the Welsh Office gave its decision. 'Welsh Office Axe Falls on A5 Schemes,' was the headline in *Construction News*, the builders' newspaper, and the text continues:

> The Welsh Office has pulled the plug on £27 million-worth of road construction schemes along the route of the A5 in north Wales. Among the projects are the £6 million Padog Bends improvement, where the landowner, the National Trust, was threatening to oppose the scheme in Parliament; the £8 million Bethesda bypass, the £6 million Halfway Bridge improvement and the Llangollen bypass.
>
> The roads' lobby suspect the move is another example of a government inspired cost-cutting exercise, but Welsh Roads Minister, Gwilym Jones said, "The A5 winds its way through the National Park, and in deciding the road's future, environmental consideration was crucial."

And the *Daily Post* added in its report on the announcement:

> The Welsh Office axed the massive A5 plans to protect the rural beauty of north Wales. For the first time the Snowdonia countryside was given precedence over the drive for faster traffic and the Bethesda and Llangollen bypasses were axed. The announcement was cheered by environmental, wildlife and countryside groups who had campaigned for years against turning the A5 into a Euro route.

The trunk road was then given the title 'The A5 Historic Route' with brown signs all the way from Chirk to Llandegai.

* * *

The annual plant sale at Dyffryn continued to thrive, but the tenth and final sale was arranged by Esmé and Peter in 1991. It had grown into a three-day event and when the treasurer finished counting the amount received in the 1991 sale, the final total was £10,300. This took fundraising for the capital fund beyond the goal of £50,000, the formidable sum which had been set by Esmé ten years earlier. The enterprise in 1991 was more than just a financial success; the weather for the three days was glorious too. Members had given up their time months earlier to pot up plants, bake, distribute sale notices, do the publicity and get everything ready. Esmé and Peter hoped that their last plant sale enterprise would go out on a high. And so it did, and at the end of the three days, David Firth paid a fulsome tribute to Esmé and Peter for their commitment, enthusiasm and stamina in staging the event for ten years. He also announced that the enterprise would continue, but under new management.

David Firth also encouraged another project to mark the Society's twenty-fifth year. 'Operation Eyesore' involved young people predominantly. Schools were contacted in the first instance, asking pupils to list local eyesores, but only one letter was received in response. David Firth thought again; he drew up his own list of eyesores, one for every year of the Society's existence. This time, schools were contacted to suggest ways of improving and dealing with eyesores, such as litter, old machinery, rotting fences, fly-tipping and many more. This scheme caught the imagination and, year by year, other eyesores were suggested and removed by young people.

A bilingual magazine, *Eryri*, was a new venture by the Society. It added another means of communicating with people interested in the well-being and activities of the National Park. It developed from a newsletter into an attractive and stylish informative magazine with stunning photographs. Two editions a year evolved into three, containing news from the Park Authority, profiles of those working in the Park and erudite articles written by those who visited the Park to speak at themed conferences and meetings.

Despite all the good ideas and the hard work behind the scenes, Esmé's autocratic attitude and interference still caused friction, undermining the work of the new executive, provoking instability and causing a split within committees. A few left, while the chairman attempted to steer the Society's affairs once again, going through the process of appointing yet another new director.

The Society had a staff of three by now. Around the Tŷ Hyll headquarters Pam and Neville Jones led groups of enthusiastic volunteers who worked on the cottage garden. In the process, a great deal of buried rubbish was found and Neville Jones noted, 'All needing removal before plants can feel comfortable'. Esmé was enthusiastic about the planting project around Tŷ Hyll. She supervised thousands of daffodils being planted in the woodland; with bluebells, primroses and violets already established. 'Hardy cyclamen, anemone blanda, dog's tooth violet and other colourful spring flowers. This garden should enhance the Ugly House and encourage visitors to return, saying as so many have already, it is not ugly; it is beautiful.'

12

I N HIS FIRST annual report Martyn Evans remarked on the good relationship he'd developed with the National Park Authority. He also noted that David Firth had also begun to establish contact with the Council of National Parks. All three National Parks in Wales and the National Parks of England had watchdog societies. The Council of National Parks arranged a two-day seminar in Llanberis for representatives of all Park watchdogs to exchange ideas and information and to learn from successes and failures. One session of particular interest was learning how individual Societies work effectively with other agencies to promote stronger legislation for National Parks (a proposition that Esmé had often dealt with on her own – an aspect of Esmé's leadership – leading from the front but without consultation).

Martyn Evans also revealed that the Society had received a request from the Park Authority for opinions on at least forty planning applications. These were extremely complex and, as a result, decision were made frustratingly slow. The Government had simplified the procedures for applying for planning permission, by providing a single plan adhering to legal conditions so that they would not be so complex, and this proved a major shift of emphasis.

David Firth's first annual report in 1992 described the application made for a Hydro-Electric Scheme for Fairy Glen, Betws-y-coed, a popular beauty spot within the Park. This proposal had generated considerable debate. The trustees of the Foelas Estate wanted to draw water from the River Conwy, allowing it to fall via a four-foot pipe to a turbine house near the Fairy Glen Hotel. Electricity would then be generated and sold to the National Grid to supply seven hundred homes and water would be pumped back into the river.

This scheme did not have the usual 'jobs vs environment' argument as it was to be entirely mechanised. Not only the community, but the wider population would have a supply of renewable energy. The Society set out its concerns about the proposal:

> The level of water taken from the River Conwy would have a detrimental effect on the ecology of the river.
> The visual impact of the turbine house from the A470.
> The scheme contained a request to fell broadleaved trees although they were on private land.

Following many visits and meetings, the Society wrote to the Park Authority:

> We point out that the Society is generally in favour of renewable energy production and broadly in support of this scheme. It is, however, vital that great care is taken over details because of the sensitivity of this site. The level of water abstraction is the most critical aspect. They intend drawing over one third of the River Conwy's flow at certain times. This is bound to have an effect on the ecology of the river (a Site of Special Scientific Interest) and we suggest that in view of this, it is premature to grant planning consent.

The application for the scheme was eventually withdrawn as it proved impossible to resolve the issues raised. But there were other similar schemes in the pipeline causing concern too, and Gwynedd County Council commissioned environmental consultants to conduct a landscape survey to assess other suitable energy schemes and their potential impact on the landscape.

* * *

Any group which campaigns has a bulging 'pending' file of plans waiting to be resolved. Letters and reports dealing with on-going sagas soon accumulated as the Park Authority had no legislative powers on major schemes. The most difficult and long-lasting project was the effect of noise from power boats, and water-skiing on Llyn Geirionydd, the only one of the sixty-seven lakes in Snowdonia which allowed such activity. As mentioned earlier, noise pollution at the lake was first raised by the Society at their second meeting in 1969 and little did they think their protestations would continue for four decades.

Back then Esmé believed that Caernarfon County Council should make bye-laws against this. But progress was slow. The Park Authority, the County Council, the Countryside Commission, the Welsh Office and the Home Office seemed unable to find an answer either, as noted in the Society's 1975, 1977 and 1979 reports.

In 1984 Esmé felt that the Welsh language was the issue for the delay in progress and wrote, 'There is a language problem between the Home Office and Gwynedd County Council. The Home Office insist that English must be used on all legal documents, the County Council is equally insistent that Welsh must take precedence. The public is not much bothered either way, they wanted the noise to stop and to leave Geirionydd peaceful and tranquil.'

As the Society approached its fortieth birthday in 2007, an Environment Agency report found that bathers and picnickers made more noise than power boats and the Park Authority decided that 'managed use' was preferable to a ban. Today the level of noise in summer months continues to hover over the Carneddau range and the Conwy Valley for those people who come to Snowdonia looking for solitude.

* * *

Folllowing the 1991 annual general meeting which heralded the transition between the old and new leadership, Esmé often made her presence felt in the office and at meetings. She had little or no faith in the new leadership and would speak openly to her friends criticizing the Society for going in the wrong direction. The new constitution took a long time to formalize; it was a detailed document which would need to cover all aspects and issues without ambiguity. The executive had already decided that documents placed in the public domain should be bilingual. Another major change put forward to members at the 1992 annual general meeting was a change to the Society's title, from The Snowdonia National Park Society to The Snowdonia Society – short and crisp, concise in both languages and not to be confused with the National Park Authority, as was the tendency in the past.

As time went by Esmé felt she was losing her grip on the Society, realising her status had diminished. She questioned decisions and disagreed with the new policies, actions which seemed to be attempting to undermine David Firth. Esmé was no longer a strong physical presence, she was well into her eighties, stooping and looking frail, and annoyed with her failing body. It would not behave as she wanted it to, to carry on being fiery, feisty, active – just as she was when she first arrived at Dyffryn – but the fighting spirit was maybe misguided and prevented her adapting to change.

* * *

However, Martyn Evans found the pressure of the post of director too much and, after eighteen months, he left for a job with the Countryside Council for Wales. He had been a breath of fresh air, enthusiastic and hard working. Despite Esmé's interference he organised a new competition, as already mentioned, the Eryri Farming and Landscape Award, in an attempt to encourage the farmers of the area to be involved with the Society. There was much interest in this competition and the judges assessed six farms, with the first winner being a 300-acre farm with 545 ewes, Cefn Cymerau Ucha, Llanbedr, which overlooked Cardigan Bay. Conservation had been promoted for many years on this farm, and its features included a nature walk, lake, new dry-stone walls, new buildings, one of which was used for lambing in spring and was the occasional setting for a *noson lawen*, an evening of traditional of Welsh light entertainment, in summer.

Evans was followed in post by Rory Francis, a Welsh speaker who had been a researcher in the House of Commons and had campaigned for Friends of the Earth. He was soon involved in the 'Right to Roam' debate which educated the public to respect the mountain landscape. There had been a steady increase in the number of new visitors to the countryside who had roamed wherever they liked. There was a need for visitors to be educated to keep to the designated paths.

The two years of David Firth's chairmanship were torrid, especially after Martyn Evans's early departure. Esmé would encourage another candidate to lead the Society but twice her ploy failed. The third time, in 1994, Esmé and her close supporters called for a special general meeting to debate a motion of no confidence in the chairman. In a packed hall in Llanrwst, the motion was overwhelmingly defeated. Despite widespread admiration for Esmé's achievements, members of the Society had had enough of her meddling.

At this final defeat Esmé was wounded and damaged. She withdrew from the Society altogether and her husband resigned from the committee. Peter had been her rock through these uncomfortable times, and he had prepared her for the fall, knowing that Esmé had been living in the hope that the membership would carry her back to the chairmanship. She and Peter sat through that meeting not allowing their emotions to surface. The former actress had shown presence and toughness.

David Firth had brought change to the Society. This he had done with dignified leadership, raising the Society's status. However, these few, short years had taken their toll. David's health deteriorated and he handed the reins after one four-year term to Jenny Nickson, née James, who had been the Society's administrator ten years earlier.

* * *

Despite withdrawing completely from the Society, Peter and Esmé were not idle. Esmé felt there was more work to do for Snowdonia and the couple opened another chapter with a new charity. The Esmé Kirby Snowdonia Trust had been registered with the Charity Commission as early as 1990. They had also been discussing personal matters for some time, especially the future of Dyffryn after their days. Esmé had lived there for sixty-five years, hoping for a few more to come, but her real desire was that it remained a working mountain sheep farm after her time. They both agreed that they should bequeath the two houses to the National Trust in the hope that Geraint Roberts would stay on as the tenant for the new land owners. Detailed plans for the couple's wills and bequests began.

13

E SMÉ HAD LONG admired the work of the National Trust, in particular their respect for the Snowdonia landscape and the ancient farming practices of the mountain terrain. She had a warm friendship with Fiona Reynolds from the time when she was the secretary for the Council of National Parks, to the time when she joined the National Trust as its director.

Dame Fiona visited Dyffryn many times and David Firth commented, 'Fiona Reynolds would be happy to admit that Esmé was one of those people who was an inspiration to her. She came to speak at the dinner held at Henllys Hall, Beaumaris, to celebrate the Society's twenty-first anniversary in 1988 and also to recognise the leadership and pioneering work of its founder.' At that celebratory dinner Esmé was given £3,500 from collections and donations made by members of the Society. It was thought that she might buy a piece of land or woodland with the money, which would forever associate her name with the Society.

But it was at this time that a few close friends and leaders of other organisations started to hint that she should retire from the chairmanship. Esmé also realised too that she didn't command total respect in the Society any longer. Approaching her eighties, and without telling the Society, she decided that the £3,500 was to be used to establish a trust fund for Snowdonia in her name with the Charity Commission.

The Esmé Kirby Snowdonia Trust Fund signed by Esmé Kirby, and, R. J. Collett and W. J. Irving, on 1 February 1990. The trustees have raised the sum of £5,120 and intend to raise other funds and gifts and the objectives are:

a) To advance the education of the public by the preservation, protection and improvement of the Snowdonia National Park.
b) To provide bursaries and grants to students working in the field of conservation.

The first two trustees were family relatives, husbands of her two nieces Jenny and Val. Given the above date, Esmé and Peter must have taken the decision to establish the Trust some considerable time before the date when she lost the vote for the leadership of the Snowdonia National Park Society in October 1991.

I asked David Firth for his reaction when he realised that the £3,500 was to be used to establish a Trust in her name for Snowdonia, and not to buy a piece of land. 'I was embarrassed. I knew there was friction between committee members who had been elected. Many left and Esmé filled the places with her friends. Unfortunately, another facet of her personality surfaced when her tenacity and stubbornness emerged, she could not give up her executive role, and this became the period when Esmé lost her graciousness.'

Before finalizing plans to create the Esmé Kirby Snowdonia Trust Fund, she had called many close friends and sought their advice. A few of these friends were added to the list of trustees: Peter, her husband; Bob Lowe, a senior planner for the Park Authority and Colonel Jonathan Cox, a military man of the Marches. According to Esmé, the aims were simply: 'It is to be a truly voluntary organisation. If people work for or give to the Trust they do so because they love Snowdonia. Any individual, society or organisation can apply to the Trust for funds for any scheme that would increase the enjoyment, protection or enhancement of the irreplaceable landscape of Snowdonia. We hope to act as a catalyst for voluntary effort in Snowdonia.'

The trustees thought that a large capital sum was essential if the Trust was to be effective. They decided on a target of £100,000. Some thought it far too ambitious but they were proved wrong. The response to their appeal was instant. By mid-July 1995, £10,000 had been raised and at the end of the year the capital fund had reached £40,000. It was gratifying and heart warming for Esmé. She recorded, 'There is something about Snowdonia. Once experienced, always loved and many letters emphasised that affection.'

Her devotion to the mountains had not wavered, and forming another Trust in direct competition with an established Society with very similar objectives was a manifestation of her stubborn nature and rebelliousness. She was determined to lead a small, effective organisation from the front, with trustees who were her friends and peers. There were no committees, no paid officials and she set her own agenda. She was an autocratic leader who got on with the work. She commanded respect for her past achievements but now, largely replicating the aims of her first society, she had perhaps taken a step too far.

Her Trust fund would deal with these projects:

1. To establish a low-level walk from Capel Curig to Pen-y-Gwryd and return by the bank of the River Gwryd.
2. New path from Nant Peris car park and Pen-y-Pass.
3. Removing ten minor eyesores from Snowdonia every year. The trustees intend to wage war on all graffiti in Gwynedd, remove the isolated dump of tarmac near Llyn Gwynant and a large pile of used silage bags on a roadside.
4. Planting with grass the stone embankment at the top of Nant Gwynant near Pen-y-Gwryd.
5. Reopening of the old railway track between Bala and Trawsfynydd.

6. Tir Stent, or the worst eyesore in the Park.
7. We asked, 'Where have all the little birds gone?'
8. Repair the boggy section of the path from Bronaber to Llanbedr via Roman steps.
9. The footbridge over the River Llugwy to connect the Crafnant Path with the old road from Capel Curig to Ogwen.

It was a daunting list, given that two of the trustees were octogenarians. Esmé and Peter were already enthusiastically involved in the work of the Trust: letter writing, seeking out volunteers and making sure financial targets were on course. Esmé was having a new lease of life; she was in control and content, and was able to record at the end of the first year of establishment of the Esmé Kirby Snowdonia Trust, 1995, 'We are reasonably pleased with progress.'

But there were delays on work at the low-level walk from Capel Curig to Pen-y-Pass, because the army, who were to survey the route and build bridges, was deployed overseas to Bosnia and was unable to help. The Countryside Council of Wales had also had a large cut in its budget and, until they assessed their situation, they were forced to withdraw their financial support temporarily.

However, Peter contacted his former battalion, the Royal Welch Fusiliers, and met Major David Snape, who turned out to be a qualified surveyor. He volunteered to map the eight-mile section. It was a turning point and the volunteers began their work, building and erecting seventeen bridges and fifteen stiles made by the Park Authority. Determination, stamina, goodwill and the cooperation of many people meant that Esmé's promise was fulfilled. The opening ceremony of the low-level walk was conducted by Chris Brasher on 31 August 1996. It was a splendid success and Cllr John Tudor, chairman of the Park Authority, praised the trustees for their initiative in making a path on private land available to the public (most of the land was owned by Esmé). One hundred and seventy spectators walked with Chris and Esmé to the first stile and, with one swipe, Chris cut the climbing rope across the top step and announced that the Dyffryn low-level walk was open.

Esmé prepared a booklet for the first-time walkers of this path. The introduction began:

> It is a walk for those who do not wish to climb the heights and for those whose legs are, as yet, too short to do so. Whenever you are on the mountains you are the guest of the hill farmer and when you climb over the first stile on your walk around Dyffryn Mymbyr, you become the guest of farmer Geraint Roberts. From here his land covers [over] 3,000 acres of the southern slopes of the two Glyderau and down to the River Gwryd in the valley below. It carries a permanent flock of breeding ewes and a hundred cattle. With ewes, yearling ewes and lambs the number increases to nearly 4,000 in the summer.

The twelve-page narrative describes the farming year, the husbandry of sheep and cattle, the terrain, the buildings (houses and barns), the gathering, dipping, shearing of sheep and the role of the open mountain and how sheep instinctively know not to wander. However, it does not mention the other farms in the valley, Garth and Cwm, the two working farms on the foothills of Moel Siabod.

The booklet ends with a comment on the hard work of the farmer's life, '… maintaining some eighteen miles of walls and fences, over a hundred gates and twelve buildings. Geraint and his son Glyn are modern hill farmers. Life is still hard but they love the mountains and their sheep. As long as there are people like them, the hills will prosper.'

The walk was not the only project completed at that time. They tackled Tir Stent, the so-called worst eyesore in the Park, which had been so for twenty-five years. An old quarry called Tir Stent was part of the common land above Dolgellau, and was regularly used by the public to dump old fridges, cookers, mattresses, bicycles and many other items of household rubbish. It was within the Park but the responsibility of Meirionnydd District Council, initially. For years the illicit tip grew and grew. In 1995 the Park Authority offered the council £3,000 towards clearing it, but the offer was turned down as it was estimated that it would cost well into five figures.

Esmé took the trustees to inspect the site and told the District Council that the Trust could accomplish 'a much less costly approach'. The Park Authority was happy to accept the estimate and, at her beguiling best she told them, 'I know a man with a JCB'. Meirionnydd District Council eventually approved the clearance.

Volunteers moved in and in a few days they reported 'job done'. The site was reseeded and in the spring a Mountain Ash sapling tree was planted there. So impressed were the authorities that they offered a small grant to remove another tip, Upper Pant Wood, also near Dolgellau. Nine volunteers from RAF Cosford, organised by Gwyn Owen of the Park Authority, set to work and in no time they had removed all the bulky rubbish, and a farmer with a large trailer carried it to the roadside ready for removal by the District Council. A JCB moved in and covered the area with a thick layer of soil in readiness for spring.

Another project completed was repairing two boggy sections of another path, from Bronaber near Trawsfynydd to Llanbedr. The path was the responsibility of Forest Enterprise and Gwynedd County Council. There was immediate cooperation from those authorities and according to one walker, 'We were amazed at the transformation, two years ago it was a slog; this year a pleasurable walk.'

Other projects needed attention too and joined the list, but one or two were long-term issues. The Telford Milestones on the A5 highway was a special project. Esmé and Peter had taken many journeys to and from Capel Curig to Bangor and Holyhead. This was a section of road that Thomas Telford had built from London to Holyhead in seven years and was opened in 1819. The Irish Mail stagecoach would cover the journey from London to Holyhead in just over twenty-four hours, and every fifteen miles it would change horses. Telford placed massive granite stones as markers along the route. Fixed to each stone was an iron plate showing the number of miles to Holyhead and the number of miles and furlongs to the next milestone. Every changeover of horses was swift, on a point of honour not to delay the mail coach. Esmé and Peter located every stone between Llangollen and Holyhead, only seven were missing out of the seventy-seven, and across the Park and Anglesey only three iron plates were missing.

Esmé and Peter had been working on the milestone project for twenty years or more. Initially they wrote to the Welsh Office to request a grant to replace the iron plates. A reply on 29 September 1982 indicated that they would get a grant, but it was to be a long wait. The devolution referendum of 1997 took place, with a transfer of powers from Westminster to Scotland, Wales and Northern Ireland, resulting in a parliament in Edinburgh and assemblies in Cardiff and Belfast. Five years later the Department for the Environment allocated £50,000 to the project, but sadly Esmé had died before the agreement was honoured. Work began on the A5 highway and every Telford Milestone was slowly put in place but, for Peter, it was a bittersweet celebration.

* * *

In the first Trust annual report in 1995 Esmé posed the question, 'Where have all the little birds gone? The tits, robins, wrens, finches and ground nesting birds, larks, lapwings, curlew, snipe, corn and reed bunting, some on the endangered list, but the increasing magpie population plays a part in their declining numbers. The vicious attacks on the eggs and fledglings of little birds are well known.'

Esmé and Peter began using traps and they caught thirty-six magpies at their first attempt, in addition to a few crows and grey squirrels. They believed that there should be a balance in nature, and trapping could assist the quest to protect the weak and vulnerable.

And that was also true of the indigenous red squirrels, which were rapidly disappearing from woodlands, and, on Anglesey, they were on the point of extinction. The grey squirrels had been introduced to south-west England over a hundred years earlier. Initially, reds and greys settled well together, although both species could be bad tempered. They did not interbreed, though they used each others' nests, dreys, though not at the same time. The reds are herbivores and the greys omnivores, but early observers noted that whenever the greys established themselves, the reds disappeared at an alarming rate. Esmé took the message to her trustees and, although Anglesey was outside the Park, they were unanimous that, as conservationists, they were ready to 'Make Anglesey, once again, red squirrel country.'

14

THE TRUSTEES OF the Esmé Kirby Snowdonia Trust felt slightly guilty when they decided to switch their main focus to Anglesey, and it was a sentiment underlined in their report which stated, 'That every penny donated to the Trust would be spent on Snowdonia, but if the Anglesey Red Squirrel Project succeeded, it would be a considerable triumph.' Esmé and Peter were already committed, indeed galvanised.

Lady Anglesey, the Marchioness of the island's Plas Newydd Estate, had read the Trust's 1996 report and she offered her support. She agreed to chair a small meeting of representatives from organisations on the island who were also showing interest in the cause. Their reactions were practical and resolute, and it was evident that Esmé had found another 'cause' and was ready to get things moving. Firstly, she and Peter visited the Red Squirrel Research for English Nature project in Formby, Lancashire, and there they met the scientist, Dr Craig Shuttleworth. His memory of Esmé at that first meeting at Easter 1997 is:

'She was very persuasive and I agreed to help. I was coming to the end of a contract and I was about to lose the house, they wanted it back. "OK," I said, "if you can get me somewhere to stay." She took half a second to think. "Leave it with me," she said. The next night she phoned, she'd found somewhere. "When can you start?" And I said, "I'll start at the beginning of January at the end of this piece of work." And I sort of realised that Esmé hadn't told her newly-established project members about the action she'd just taken. She just employed me... how, I don't know, a number were very pleased, others said, "Hold on a minute!" But she wanted to hit the ground running.'

I met Craig Shuttleworth over ten years later; he is an enthusiastic academic with a deep love of the countryside and red squirrels, and he and his family have settled well in Wales. His passion for saving and protecting red squirrels matched Esmé's; they had a similar outlook:

'I was a student really, a graduate of Edinburgh University, in wildlife management. I'd just finished my PhD and I turned up as I am now, really scruffy. Esmé talked and talked, she wanted to clear the island of grey squirrels and I smiled and thought, that's quite a challenge. She knew what she wanted; she knew the path she wanted to follow and if there were people who didn't want that, they had to have a pretty good reason to stop her because the project was going to happen. She always looked for ways to make things happen anyway. I went to Anglesey and talked to many people about the Esmé Kirby Snowdonia Trust and I got many reactions. Some said, "Oh, you'll enjoy that!" Others looked at me as though a cloud had gone over the sun – you're going to work with *her*? Rather you than me mate. But those in the past who may have had a disagreement with her recognised her passion and went along with the project.'

The grey squirrels had become destructive pests: they ate food put out for little birds, eggs and young birds in nests, bulbs planted in gardens, all soft fruit, and also nuts before they were ripe. Their sharp teeth seemed to cope with wood, wiring and plumbing, and they were the curse of every forester as they ate young shoots and were able to strip bark from mature trees, even. The greys were classified officially as a pest in 1981, and anyone who caught a grey on their land had to notify the Department of Agriculture, a statute which was part of the Grey Squirrel Act. The aim of the Trust was to reduce the number of greys so that they were no longer a nuisance and would allow more red squirrels to return to the countryside.

Within months the red squirrel project committee organised a conference at Plas Newydd to hear the results of Dr Suttleworth's survey and to listen to the advice of John Gurnell, a leading authority on red squirrels, and Harry Pepper of the Forestry Commission. The committee then worked out a five-year plan. In the first two years they would try to reduce the grey squirrel population in the east of the island and on the mainland opposite (the greys were well able to use the two bridges and, if necessary, they could swim across the Menai Straits). In the third year they hoped to encourage the small indigenous population of reds which had survived the grey invasion.

It would be a costly project but the Esmé Kirby Snowdonia Trust had already promised to fund Dr Shuttleworth for the first six months after January 1998. They would then have to wait for the remaining funds from other Government agencies, such as the Countryside Council for Wales and Menter Môn. In addition, two members of the committee established the Friends of the Anglesey Red Squirrel to liaise among local people. So, by this time, the project committee led by Lady Anglesey was gaining a reputation for being formidable and determined to accomplish its aims.

Craig Shuttleworth began work as agreed in January but the project was in danger of losing momentum because of what Esmé called 'bureaucratic obstacles – who does what and who pays for it'. Two months passed before they could begin trapping using live cage traps on the east of the island (Pentraeth), where there was a small colony of between twelve and twenty red squirrels, the survivors.

There had been many schemes to cull the greys in the past, such as offering a sixpence or a shilling for a grey squirrel tail, but those had failed. Initially metal traps were bought but they were difficult to use and too small. So Peter Kirby designed a wooden box with a seesaw at the entrance – when the squirrel stepped inside, the seesaw closed the trap.

Never a particularly patient woman, Esmé was anxious to see action; there had been too many delays and she wanted farmers and landowners to be kept informed. She told Craig, 'Go and see Edna, she'll help you, this is about getting the job done – there are mounds of paperwork and strategies that so often achieve very little, they waste time. We need to get rid of as many grey squirrels as we can.'

In 1964 Edna and her husband David had moved from a large 1,000-acre mountain farm in Snowdonia to the milder climate of Anglesey, and a much smaller 160-acre farm. They kept a small flock of sheep and herd of beef cattle. David had died a few years before my visit and when I met Edna she had vivid memories of the 1950s, learning sheep farming on the mountains with her late husband and Esmé.

Edna knew that there were many people on Anglesey who objected to the cull of greys. Some felt it was frightfully cruel to kill the 'darling little greys' but Edna's response was that they'd be replacing them with 'darling little reds'. Edna had taken the cue from Esmé; she too was straight, forthright and unafraid of treading on toes. The timing of the most high-profile objection to the trapping of greys, from the Wildlife Trust, coincided with Esmé's proposal to try to resurrect the aforementioned forestry scheme, and pay a £1 per grey squirrel tail. She told Lady Anglesey, 'I would like to do it,' and Lady Anglesey replied, 'If you want to do it, you do it,' and Esmé looked at her, and said emphatically, 'I will.'

Everyone realised that eliminating all the grey squirrels in England and Wales would be impossible – the estimate was 2.5 million – but other areas could replicate the Anglesey campaign. Using humane live cage traps, 2,500 greys were removed from the Pentraeth area of Anglesey. The number of red squirrels subsequently increased dramatically when a grey-free zone was established in and around the Pentraeth Forest. There the reds began breeding and by autumn 1998 the population increased to sixty. The trapping was extended to the Plas Newydd Estate and a further 2,000 greys were removed, with the reds soon establishing themselves there too. By the turn of the millennium the reds were returning to other woodland areas of the island.

* * *

A decade later, and I'm enjoying a mug of tea with Craig and Edna at her farm above Beaumaris, listening to the account of the campaign, when a voice calls from the back door. 'Hello! It's £45, Edna. That Digger did a bl***y good job, didn't it?'

Edna goes to the kitchen to give the money to Tom, a neighbour who helped her with heavy work. He turns to Craig and asks, 'How are you Craig? Very good?' And Craig says he is in fine fettle when Tom's voice, full of enthusiasm adds, 'They've seen three red squirrels in the village at the bungalows, you know. Three up there and two at the school as well.'

'Oh super,' says Craig, clasping his hands together, and Tom takes a step nearer, 'Oh yes, they're coming down, they're coming down all right! It's good news.'

'Good news indeed. Two at the school. It's good because we do a lot of work with schools.'

* * *

Esmé wrote to every school in Anglesey as she wanted them to get involved in the red squirrel campaign. Craig noted, 'They embraced it. You know they raised the money and we did educational talks and gave instructional plans of how we were, at last, improving things by introducing the reds to woodlands in new localities such as the Llangefni Dingle and you see they've become part of the fabric of the landscape of the island. That was Esmé's vision.'

The sighting of those squirrels in Llangefni meant that the reds had arrived on the western side of the island and the early years' work had been effective. In Newborough Forest 498 greys were removed in 2002; 34 removed in 2003; 0–10 removed in 2004–10.

In recent times the disease squirrelpox, a form of flu, has hit the red squirrel population hard. Sores in the eyes, ears and mouth can cause death within three weeks. Another virus, adenovirus, which caused lesions in the intestine, struck the reds in 2011 and caused death in three days. These viruses swept through the colonies of reds and sixty-five per cent of them perished, but the grey squirrels, which carried the viruses, survived.

Two colonies of red squirrels settled in the broadleaved woodland at Plas Newydd, much to the pleasure of Lady Anglesey. In conjunction with the Moredun Research Institute, Craig Shuttleworth began a major project to discover a vaccine for squirrelpox – the estimated cost was £408,000. They had already received a substantial sum from the Wildlife Ark Trust so that the research work could commence, and the Friends of the Red Squirrel Trust in Anglesey, led by Dr Raj Jones, was determined to make up the difference and applied to the Heritage Lottery Fund. The application was successful and the Red Squirrel Trust was awarded £300,000. Craig Shuttleworth announced, 'Of all the conservation initiatives, I consider the squirrelpox vaccine research the one most likely to be the saviour of the red squirrels.'

* * *

When Esmé began the squirrel project in 1997 she didn't forget the Trust's other projects. She set her sights on another pest, the magpie, hence the title of one of the projects in her first report for the Trust, 'Where have all the little birds gone?'

This project was an immediate success. Using the local press to outline her concerns, over five hundred people replied to give their support to the culling of magpies using the humane Larsen trap. For the cost of £5 to cover expenses, she posted out a kit with comprehensive instructions and the essential springs. These traps eliminated a thousand magpies and were an excellent launch-pad for the nationwide official Magpie Campaign which began on 1 March 1997. Those buying the trap would also join the Anti-Magpie Brigade.

However, not everyone was happy. The British Trust for Ornithology (BTO) and the Royal Society for the Protection of Birds (RSPB) didn't want anything to do with the campaign. There was disbelief from people who had a bird table in their garden. W.F. Deedes, former editor of the *Daily Telegraph*, received nine letters in reply to an article, 'Magpies, the evidence of their guilt'. One of the letters came from a veterinary surgeon who responded to a report by the BTO and the RSPB saying: 'It illustrates once again the triumph of quasi-science over common sense... If scientists could be persuaded to become naturalists, we, who know better, might be more impressed by their findings.'

Esmé, in her report, emphasised again that they had no wish to eliminate these handsome but vicious birds: 'But we are determined to send it back where it belongs and out of our gardens. It is a woodland bird. It will continue to eat little birds, that is nature's way. Whatever the size, the stronger always prey upon their weaker brethren but we would like our little garden birds to have a better chance of survival.'

Esmé and Peter treasured a greeting they received on a Christmas card that year: 'A happy Christmas, with thanks from the little birds.'

* * *

The Trust's 1998 report included the headline, THE GREAT SNOWDON (FARM) SALE. This had caused panic stations in May because the press (local, national and international) had written headlines suggesting that Snowdon was for sale. The fear was that the first to bid £3 to £4 million would become the owner of the 4,000-acre farm on the slopes of Snowdon, Hafod y Llan, and the adjacent farm, Gelli Iago. Gossip spread up and down the mountain that a wealthy foreign gentleman might buy and exploit it. A Cardiff consortium made the first bid for the farm but soon dropped out and, a few weeks later, the National Trust announced that, with public help, it would try to raise the money needed to buy the farm. Owner Richard Williams was persuaded to agree to this, but made a proviso that the sale would have to be completed within a hundred days.

Hafod y Llan was tucked on the floor of the Nant Gwynant Valley and had been in the Williams family for generations. Richard Williams had inherited the sheep farm with its land which rose to 3,560 feet and included the summit of Snowdon. The National Trust were persuaded to show an interest in the farm as a result of its symbolic location, conservation factors (it was a National Nature Reserve and SSSI), its Grade II listed buildings and rural upland heritage. One of Snowdon's most famous paths, the Watkin Path, passed through the private land of Hafod y Llan, but when the path was officially opened by Prime Minister Gladstone in 1892, it was designated a public path. Standing on the now-famous Gladstone Rock that day, the Prime Minister spoke at such length that he almost forgot to declare the path open!

The National Trust's appeal to purchase the farm was launched and money came in, in large and small amounts, including a generous sum from the Prince of Wales. The Welsh actor Sir Anthony Hopkins donated £1 million. Within a hundred days the funds needed had been raised due to the emotive appeal: Snowdon belonged to Wales; it must be saved. Therefore, the National Trust added another well-endowed 4,000 acres to its 50,000-acre Snowdonia estate.

The National Trust's aim for its farms in Snowdonia was to re-introduce traditional farming techniques in a progressive bid to face up to issues such as habitat decline, the halving of sheep numbers, and the introduction of conservation projects.

Today the financial viability of farms in Snowdonia has become uncertain, with farmers relying increasingly on grants and subsidies. Richard Williams now has a home overlooking Llyn Dinas and a business on Anglesey. He was pessimistic when I met him. 'It is difficult to think about the future in Snowdonia. The bottom line in farming up here in the mountains is finished in this kind of environment. The farm opposite, Llyndy Isaf, was put up for sale for £1 million and the National Trust is appealing once again, but I'm not sure how long they're going to persuade people to chase sheep from the mountains.'

Farmer Ken Owen of Llyndy Isaf changed his farming emphasis a few years before he decided to sell and retire. He sought advice from the Park Authority as he was looking for a sustainable living. They recommended that he develop his campsite and encourage recreation, protect the farm's wildlife habitats and manage the rampant rhododendrons. He got rid of most of his sheep on his 614 acres, and allowed the land to regenerate trees and scrub, and spent his days driving his livestock wagon instead. According to Richard Williams, 'It was Ken Owen's pride and joy – he was allowed to do what he always wanted to do – drive his wagon here and there to markets and meet people. He would have had to keep four to five hundred sheep to carry on, to sustain a living.' The time had now come for Owen to retire completely, and he approached the National Trust with a view to selling the farm. Richard Williams added, 'The landscape at Llyndy Isaf had become very different without the sheep. The trees have slowly regenerated. There's bio-diversity in the mountains, the pastoral tradition today is another story. Is it financially viable if it relies on grants and payments? There is no safety net in the mountains. You just batten down the hatches and get on with things.'

The National Trust's appeal to raise £1 million to buy Llyndy Isaf was successful and it prevented commercial exploitation to develop a water sports centre there. Llyndy Isaf is thought to be the setting of a mythical battle between a red and a white dragon. The legend says that the red dragon, the conquering hero, triumphed over its adversary to become the national emblem of Wales, and the white dragon tumbled into the lake, never to be seen again.

Richard Williams was despondent about the future of farming in the mountains. 'We put Hafod y Llan up for sale, we gave up farming, the 'Right to Roam' was disabling our asset, taking the value away from what you've got. I'm a great believer in allowing people to come to the countryside to walk, but not to erode property rights, I think that's wrong. Farming is finished in these mountains, in this environment. That's the bottom line. It's a hard life.'

15

THE PAST COUPLE of years had been satisfying for the project. Craig Shuttleworth was a committed project director and, as a result, the reds were gaining ground in Anglesey. There was mutual respect between Craig and Esmé.

Other issues were not neglected, however. The Trust reminded everyone that Snowdonia's eyesores needed attention; there were footpaths to be repaired; British Telecom had promised to replace or bury the unsightly telephone poles in the Nant Ffrancon Valley, and 'tree weeds' appeared without warning and flourished. An American visitor commented to a Park officer, 'You have wonderful scenery but you can't see it for trees.'

And there was truth in the comment as, from viewing and parking places, the Mawddach estuary was hardly visible, so too the Vyrnwy reservoir and the shores of Dinas and Cnewllyn lakes. The cause was simple: self-seeding saplings were growing unchecked among the trees down to the water's edge. The Trust discussed the matter with the forestry officer, but very little action took place immediately. Stretches of the shores of various lakes and estuaries were owned by different people. However work did begin on the Mawddach estuary, in time.

News of other projects was regularly passed on to Dyffryn, and Esmé dealt with them all; the telephone conversations and letter writing continued non-stop. Approaching her nineties, she was unable to do much physical work by now. She'd begun to finalise Dyffryn's future, however. There had been many discussions with Fiona Reynolds of the National Trust, and with John Morgan, who dealt with the legal process of land acquisition and bequests for the National Trust in north Wales. Esmé had wanted all the legal side completed in 1997/8 and, by good fortune, her first husband Thomas Firbank returned to north Wales from Japan. They met for lunch and discussed many topics, though not the future of the farm, but she realised that she should be courteous and share her thoughts on Dyffryn's future with him. She wrote to him months later, in late 1997:

My Dear Thomas,
I've been meaning to write this letter for a long time. Though the objective is simple it is not so easy to put into words. Now I realise that we are running out of time, so it must be now or it may be never.
  We're both about the same age. I'm envious that you are so straight. My backbone disintegrated a bit ago and I'm dreadfully bent and look about 102. Very hurtful to my pride but fortunately the bit on the top of the chassis seems to be working OK.
  I just wanted to thank you with so much gratitude for bringing me to Dyffryn so many years ago. I can't think of a more wonderful place to have spent most of my life.
  I've thought for years of what is best for Dyffryn when I've gone. Neither you nor I have any relatives, near or distant, who could be suitable occupants. If it was put on the market and sold to the highest bidder it would, almost certainly, be broken up and sold in lots, cottages, house, parcels of land etc.
  I want and I'm sure you hope that Dyffryn will continue as a farm as you and I knew it for the foreseeable future and I have done my best to see that this happens.
  I don't want to be specific for personal reasons. You have made it a very famous farm and I would revolve in my grave if I thought I had stupidly and unwittingly not done my best to leave it in caring hands.
  I sometimes think with happy memories of our short time together here. That it was short was inevitable, neither your

fault nor mine. Perhaps more my fault – I was very naive and inexperienced and really believed that people got married and lived happily ever after and forgot all imperfections.

I've been so lucky. I've lived here for over fifty years with Peter. He loves Dyffryn and became brilliant and imaginative with everything on structure; his contribution to Dyffryn has been greater than mine. I spent most of my life shifting sheep from A to B.

Dyffryn has been a magical home.

With affectionate and happy memories,

Esmé

Time passed. There was no reply from Thomas until a letter from Japan, dated 2 February 1998:

My Dear Esmé,

Your letter to me at Dolwyddelan must be the most charming and perfectly expressed that ever passed between two humans. Thank you for it. Within the time available it will be unforgotten. I'm ashamed to have funked a reply from Wales. Time and again I failed to have justice to your quality. The attempts were cremated.

The letter then appends what he calls 'Defence of Dyffryn Mymbyr' which he explains as:

... buzz thinking which might have a skeleton bone or two toward formation of your Dyffryn Defence – a jumble of notes towards enlisting the widest support for advice:

* Sympathetic lawyer on low cost standby.
* Short hand-outs to explain self-sustaining traditional Gwynedd mountain stock farming.
* Politics. Cardiff industry-minded. Better letters, and handouts to MPs of mid and north Wales.
* Organisations – many environment bodies, National Farmers Union. Hill-walkers clubs and Rock Climbers.
* The Press – country magazines, regional, daily and local weekly papers.
* VIPs. You will certainly know a number, I only know the

Marquis of Anglesey – a tough man, good to have his
interest.

The book has been kept in print throughout the years and
decades and is still in print today. Will it live into a new
millennium with its grandly traditional subject unscathed?
Describe horrors, should multiracial entrepreneurs from the
industrial Midlands be turned loose to develop dismembered
Dyffryn.
All the very best to you both.
Thomas

Esmé must have later divulged during a phone call her
plans to bequeath the farm to the National Trust and it
triggered this response from Thomas in Japan:

14 March 1998
Dear Esmé
During our phone talk the other day thank you for letting me
hear of the plan to dispose of Dyffryn to the National Trust. As
a long-time Far East expat, I've been out of touch with Britain's
domestic affairs.

Had I thought of a National Trust I'd have pictured a self-
generated bureaucratic monster whose maw hungered for the
sustenance of crumbled mansions and mini-palaces flavoured
with dry-rot, and presented in uninspiring gardens re-laid in
basic geometrical patterns of lap computer design. Unauthorised
spasms by nature could be squared readily by rechargeable
electric clippers...

I believe Dyffryn would have settled well with enduring
mutual benefit under the auspices of a north Wales agricultural
college. From the thin scatter of whitewashed stone houses
among the steep valleys, generations of families and their litters
of tireless dogs have kept a unique style of husbandry alive from
the mountains.

Whoever or whatever gets Dyffryn gets more than a range
shaped by wrinkles in the Cambrian crust and the trim of
glaciers. Dyffryn carries with it the pattern of a region's lifestyle
from olden times if not tampered with. I like to think my

published written description of Dyffryn's lifestyle adds a value to the recipient of the property.

For this reason I have suggested a grant to the author would be appropriate.

Best wishes to you and your future.

Thomas

Firbank returned again to a Dolwyddelan hotel later in 1998 to celebrate a significant anniversary. *I Bought a Mountain* had become a literary classic and the publishers decided to present him with a special hardback edition. In another two years, the book would have been in print for sixty years. He had mentioned more than once in his letters that there was interest in making a film of the book, but it did not come to fruition. By this time Thomas's health was failing. Esmé entertained him to a lunch at Betws-y-coed and again he emphasised, 'how the book exemplifies the continuing kudos of Dyffryn' and then, he put pen to paper almost immediately:

> In the early days of World War II, I got myself sworn in as a volunteer recruit awaiting call-up for basic training in a specific sharp-end foot regiment. My future was out of my hands, but I passed to you without quibble a modernised, solid house fully furnished, well-tended and well-regarded farmland, fully stocked with great care for breeding, which I had bought before we married. My book brought you another gift, intangible but valuable. You were deliberately cast in a strong heroine role to leave you on a firm status in and outside your community. Certainly you have achieved prominence in environmental affairs.

Then, a direct demand for a return of the money that he'd paid for the remaining Dyffryn mortgage, as she hadn't revealed to him at the time that she had remarried.

Clearance was done in the belief, which your use of my surname encouraged that you were femme sole. How, as a remarried woman can you justify that mortgage demand.

I ask you now to return that sum (extrapolated to current values) for the benefit of my daughter Johanna.

It would be decent to offer some return to the Firbank family, who were fundamental in establishing Dyffryn, instead of tossing it away a very valuable and much-loved farm to an amorphous government body?

What stage are you at with the disposal of Dyffryn? What quid pro quos are involved? To what use will the two cottages and two farmhouses be put. What consideration is being given to *I Bought a Mountain* which adds so considerably to the heritage value of the farm?

Finally a number of Firbank family items, among them the family's inscribed Bible and my father's gold carriage clock, inscribed to him by my grandfather were still at Dyffryn in the 1970s. Could you please arrange for these items to be sent to the hotel?

Sincerely,

Thomas F

Esmé replied by return on 5 September 1998. She was hurt again – nearly sixty years later – but she wrote a long conciliatory letter answering all his questions:

When you bought Dyffryn around 1932 this country was in a serious depression and farming, as usual, was suffering severely, hill farming being the Cinderella of the industry even more so. After some years of effort you realised the situation and decided to leave and to look for new experiences. Then I appeared on the scene and, for a short time, my interest and enthusiasm rekindled your involvement. It didn't last. I didn't realise it [that] you were aware of the ever-increasing difficulties of making ends meet. You had to borrow twice, or was it three times, on your reversionary interest in order to keep us solvent. It didn't help that you knew one day you would inherit the Firbank estate. Our personal affairs too were a problem and made it even more essential to leave. War provided an honourable escape. You never suggested at the time, as you did over lunch some weeks ago, that one of your cousins could have come and run the farm for you. What would you have used for money? There wasn't any here and I don't think you had much either.

It's strange how old age plays havoc with memories of almost sixty years ago. The picture of Dyffryn that you carried in your mind for all these years is so very far from reality.

To some it may seem hard work, but to me it was a challenge, an exciting adventure and I loved every moment. My ambition was to make Dyffryn the best hill farm in Wales. I didn't have the qualifications but every building, house and cottage was repaired, modernised and brought to an acceptable standard. New pens were built, over a hundred gates, and some miles of new fencing were required. I soon discovered that the ewe flock was below its original numbers and it took time to build it up slowly again. All of this could only be done when time and money was available.

The last farm mortgage payment that you mention was finally paid sometime in the middle 1950s. The other mortgage payment continued to be paid on your reversionary interest until you inherited the Firbank estate, sometime, I think, in the late 1950s.

I am sorry indeed that you have had such bitter thoughts about me all these years. For some reason I always assumed that you had pleasant memories of our short time together at Dyffryn. I wrote that first letter to you because I thought you would be pleased with the arrangements I had made for the long-term future of Dyffryn after taking considerable expert advice. I didn't realise that you knew so little about the National Trust. It is the envy of every country in the Western world. It is certainly not 'an amorphous government body'.

Peter and I live here simply and very happily. My income is the rent from our tenant, plus what I have saved. Hill farming is again in the doldrums and likely to get worse, so I haven't increased the rent since I let the farm ten years ago. Fortunately, I was always a frugal spender.

The carriage clock and the family Bible were returned and she ended her letter, 'It must be a great pleasure to you that your books continue to sell so well and I do hope the proposed film is a great success.'

* * *

As far as I am aware that ends the correspondence or any contact with Firbank. Esmé and Peter were content with their transaction with the National Trust; they carried on with the red squirrel project on Anglesey, and they continued to clear other eyesores in Snowdonia. Felt pens and the typewriter were kept busy, but the physical work now was much lighter and slower. But, whatever she did, she did so with enthusiasm. She continued to attend the annual general meeting of the Snowdonia Society and the members who had berated her for establishing the Trust in direct competition to the Society had waned in their displeasure: the aim of both societies was to prevent the exploitation of Snowdonia.

16

O<small>N</small> S<small>UNDAY</small>, 17 October 1999, Esmé decided to plant daffodil bulbs in the grounds around Dyffryn, ready for the spring. It was a mellow day and when the sack of bulbs had almost emptied, she was tired and content, 'They'll be really colourful'. She retired early to bed but in the early hours of Monday, Esmé died peacefully in her sleep, aged eighty-nine, with Peter at her side.

On her desk downstairs was the fifth annual report of the trustees of the Esmé Kirby Snowdonia Trust which she'd been preparing for a meeting.

Peter fulfilled Esmé's last wish, her burial place. She had said, 'I dislike the idea of cremation, I don't want my ashes scattered.' She had chosen to be buried on a small plot of Dyffryn farmland, and Peter had to persuade the relevant authorities to give permission for this to happen. The plot she chose many years earlier overlooked the valley, and it was near the sheep pens on Glyder Fach where she had gathered and worked her flock of Welsh Mountain sheep. A moving, short service with close friends was held at the fifteenth-century St Julitta's Church, the smallest church in Snowdonia in the village of Capel Curig, followed by the burial at Dyffryn. In January 2000 there was a public thanksgiving service in her memory at St Mary's Church, Betws-y-coed, of hymns and readings.

The address was given by the Reverend Canon Michael Irving, a trustee of Esmé Kirby Snowdonia Trust. He had been an instructor at an outward bound school before becoming a rector. He recalled: 'Esmé's style was distinctive and refreshing; some found it difficult, but undoubtedly it was leadership from the front. Esmé always saw through bureaucracy and was always forthright and direct so that there were no misunderstandings. Her inspirational personality drew from us admiration, loyalty and love and she did cherish that and, at times, greatly needed it. She was indeed a heroine.'

However, there were others who remained silent, and two or three flatly refused to be interviewed for this book. There was dissent and different attitudes, but there was also quiet respect.

* * *

Peter remained at Dyffryn until he died and the trustees of the Esmé Kirby Snowdonia Trust selected him as the new chairman. He was kept busy with details of Esmé's bequest to the National Trust. He also kept in close contact with the Royal Welch Fusiliers Museum at Caernarfon Castle. Gill Richards assisted him with the administrative work of the Trust and the maintenance of stiles on the popular footpath on Dyffryn land. He was made clerk of works for the renovation work of St Julitta's Church and persuaded other trustees to agree that the Trust should partly fund the work.

When Peter reached his ninetieth birthday on 7 June 2001, a splendid lunch was served at Dyffryn followed by a surprise. Hidden behind some boulders was the goat, the goat major, and the corps of drums of the Royal Welch Fusiliers and, on a command, they marched towards the house playing 'Happy Birthday'. It was an emotional event and tears ran down Peter's cheeks. Regimental matters were still very dear to his heart.

Soldier and military historian, craftsman and conservationist, Peter had contributed in so many ways to Snowdonia and especially as help for Esmé with the administrative work for her campaigns. They were a true partnership, although many thought him subservient to his dominant wife. He carved out another life with his skill and love of craftsmanship and his interest in military history. He was a sounding board for Esmé and much more; he was always ready to discuss tricky problems and, at times, to offer the opposite view and at other times, give encouragement. As Esmé revelled in presenting her case in the spotlight on centre stage, Peter would be quietly applauding in the background with enthusiasm.

Many people were saddened when he died on 19 August 2003, aged ninety-two. His ashes were scattered next to Esmé's at Dyffryn.

* * *

In 2007 the Snowdonia Society commissioned a memorial seat made out of stone, to be placed by the water pool above Dyffryn house. The sculptor, Judy Greaves, was given the commission because she was inspired by the work that Esmé had done in Snowdonia. She chose a site which gave, '... wonderful views as well, and I shaped the seat to reflect the curves of the hillside, the lower slope of her beloved Glyder Fach. The presence of the pool also adds atmosphere.'

Esmé is resting peacefully 'at home'.

Postscript

E SMÉ AND PETER bequeathed Dyffryn to the National Trust. The farmhouse and cottage have been refurbished and modernised and, since 2010, have welcomed visitors on vacation to experience a special place in one of the most dramatic of landscapes. Esmé would be pleased that the farm's tenant, Geraint Roberts, continues to farm in an environmentally sensitive way, showing that nature conservation can be delivered on a large scale, and that upland farming can still make a profit. One fundamental shift of emphasis in the past fifteen years has been encouraging hill farmers to reduce the number of sheep and to bring back the native Welsh Black cattle.

At Dyffryn in 1967, principles were laid down by a group of friends to establish a watchdog for the National Park Authority. The basic tenets were: to preserve and enhance the natural beauty of the Park; to promote its quiet enjoyment by the public; when there was conflict, conservation should have priority, and also to cooperate with other organisations and statutory bodies to achieve this. The current director of the Snowdonia Society, John Harold, believes that these tenets are as relevant today and are as dependant on the experience and skill of the Society's members. The Society works with the National Park Authority, occasionally as an affiliated friend, and at other times, a critical one – the work by voluntary members is the key to its success.

The Esmé Kirby Snowdonia Trust, which she established when the Snowdonia Society no longer needed her leadership, has saved the red squirrel from extinction on

Anglesey. She found a leader, Dr Craig Shuttleworth, who galvanised the local community to assist the cull of the dominant grey squirrel, resulting in the colonies of reds increasing. Ten years after Esmé's death, the number of reds had reached seven hundred and the project crossed the Menai Straits to put down roots in Treboeth, Gwynedd. The red squirrel project succeeds to this day despite outbreaks of disease, and the Trust ensures that funds and assistance are forthcoming for scientific research.

Esmé's legacy? Both societies were not cosy: their members were expected to take part in activities from cleaning ditches to keeping an eye on eyesores, especially litter left on the mountains. Esmé led from the front – often it was not comfortable, but she was a lady of action who abhorred the weight of 'bureaucratic politics'.

TELERI BEVAN

The Ladies of Blaenwern

The story of The Dorian Trio
and the Llanarth Welsh Cob Stud

y Lolfa

£8.95

TELERI BEVAN

Years on Air
LIVING WITH THE BBC

£9.95